WESLEY:
A GUIDE FOR THE PERPLEXED

CONTINUUM GUIDES FOR THE PERPLEXED

Continuum's Guides for the Perplexed are clear, concise, and accessible introductions to thinkers, writers, and subjects that students and readers can find especially challenging. Concentrating specifically on what it is that makes the subject difficult to grasp, these books explain and explore key themes and ideas, guiding the reader toward a thorough understanding of demanding material.

Guides for the Perplexed **available from Continuum**
Bioethics: A Guide for the Perplexed – Agneta Sutton
Bonhoeffer: A Guide for the Perplexed – Joel Lawrence
Calvin: A Guide for the Perplexed – Paul Helm
Christian Ethics: A Guide for the Perplexed – Rolfe King
Christology: A Guide for the Perplexed – Alan J. Spence
De Lubac: A Guide for the Perplexed – David Grumett
Kierkegaard: A Guide for the Perplexed – Clare Carlisle
Martyrdom: A Guide for the Perplexed – Paul Middleton
Pannenberg: A Guide for the Perplexed – Timothy Bradshaw
Tillich: A Guide for the Perplexed – Andrew O'Neill
Trinity: A Guide for the Perplexed – Paul M. Collins
Wesley: A Guide for the Perplexed – Jason E. Vickers

WESLEY:
A GUIDE FOR THE PERPLEXED

Jason E. Vickers

t&t clark

Publishing by T&T Clark International
A Continuum Imprint
The Tower Building   80 Maiden Lane
11 York Road   Suite 704
London SE1 7NX   New York NY 10038

www.continuumbooks.com

British Library Cataloguing-in-Publication Data
A catalogue record for this book is available from the British Library

ISBN-10:   HB: 0-567-03352-X
           PB: 0-567-03353-8
ISBN-13:   HB: 978-0-567-03352-9
           PB: 978-0-567-03353-6

Typeset by Newgen Imaging Systems Pvt Ltd, Chennai, India
Printed and bound in Great Britain by MPG Books Ltd, Bodmin, Cornwall

To my parents,
for a rich Wesleyan heritage

CONTENTS

CONTENTS

ACKNOWLEDGEMENTS

I am well aware that I stand in a long line of interpreters of John Wesley, whose work I have benefited from enormously. While this line is too long to mention here, I would be remiss if I did not acknowledge William J. Abraham, Richard P. Heitzenrater and Randy L. Maddox, not only for influencing my thinking about Wesley over the years, but for giving generously of their time when questions arose during the writing of this book. I also want to thank Richard Eslinger, David Whitford and Andrew Wood for their feedback on various aspects of the work, Sarah Blair and Tom Miles for their splendid editing of the manuscript, and Evan and Julia Abla for the bibliography and index. The errors that remain are mine.

I would also be remiss if I did not acknowledge my parents, to whom this book is dedicated. Among their many gifts to me, I am especially grateful for the fact that my childhood and adolescent years were spent in the Wesleyan church and in the Church of the Nazarene, which is to say, among the Jesuits of the Wesleyan theological tradition. Moreover, I am grateful that, when the time came for me to leave home for college and then for seminary, they entrusted their son to scholars who cherished the memory and teachings of John Wesley, including Paul Bassett, Ray Dunning, Bill Greathouse, Steve Hoskins, Craig Keen, Tom Noble, Dan Spross and Rob Staples. In one way or another, I have been thinking about Wesley ever since.

Finally, I want to thank Thomas Kraft and his team at Continuum/T&T Clark. They have been timely, professional and efficient every step of the way. It has truly been a pleasure to work with them.

INTRODUCTION

What makes John Wesley so perplexing? This is a good question. At one level, he does not seem the least bit perplexing. After all, he purposely wrote in the most straightforward English prose. Moreover, he steered clear of technical, philosophical or otherwise perplexing language whenever he could. Thus, he says,

> I design plain truth for plain people. Therefore of set purpose I abstain from all nice and philosophical speculations, from all perplexed and intricate reasonings, and as far as possible from even the show of learning, unless in sometimes citing the original Scriptures. I labour to avoid all words which are not easy to be understood, all which are not used in common life; and in particular those kinds of technical terms that so frequently occur in bodies of divinity, those modes of speaking which men of reading are intimately acquainted with, but which to common people are an unknown tongue.[1]

Wesley was also clear concerning his motivation for using plain, everyday language. He intended to speak from the heart so as to be able to communicate the Gospel of Jesus Christ better.

> Nay, my design is in some sense to forget all that ever I have read in my life. I mean to speak, in the general, as if I had never read one author, ancient or modern (always excepting the inspired). I am persuaded that, on the one hand, this may be a means of enabling me more clearly to express the sentiments of my heart, while I simply follow the chain of my own thoughts, without entangling myself with those of other men; and that, on the other, I shall come with fewer weights upon my mind, with less of prejudice and prepossession, either to search for myself or to deliver to others the naked truths of the gospel.[2]

One of the assumptions behind this book is that Wesley made good on his expressed intentions to speak 'plain truth for plain people'. In many ways, Wesley is anything but perplexing. He is the sort of person who says what he means and means what he says. Consequently, his inclusion in T&T Clark's *Guides for the Perplexed* series should in no way discourage people from reading Wesley for themselves. On the contrary, in this author's judgement, lay and educated readers alike should not hesitate to dive into Wesley's sermons or even his journals and diaries. Suffice it to say, the very best way to get to know Wesley is simply to read him.

Wesley also made good on his intentions to write persuasively on behalf of the Gospel of Jesus Christ. The majority of Wesley's writings are designed either to bolster faith or to answer objections to it. On the one hand, he wrote to encourage believers and to assist them on the journey of salvation. On the other hand, he wrote to persuade non-believers by taking their objections seriously. Thus there is ample material in Wesley for believers and non-believers alike to ponder.

If Wesley is so easy to read, then why is he included in this series? More directly, what is the motivation and aim for this book? In the spirit of Wesley, I will try to answer these questions in as plain and straightforward a way as possible.

There are three things about Wesley that are especially perplexing. First, despite his insistence that he spoke 'plain truth for plain people', a rather astonishing number of interpreters have insisted that Wesley's words should not be taken at face value. There is even a tendency to see Wesley as the kind of person who said one thing and did another. For example, despite the fact that Wesley insisted that he was a 'Church of England man', that he would 'live and die' in the established Church, and that he would not leave the Church of England until his soul left his body, a wide array of scholars have argued that his actions undermined his words. Similarly, despite the fact that, in the late stages of a rather long life, Wesley declared that he was a High Church Tory and a subscriber to the Tory political doctrines of divine right and passive obedience, many scholars insist that this is, at best, only half the story. On the basis of Wesley's political writings, they insist that he was really a proto-liberal democrat.

The second thing that is perplexing about Wesley is the extent to which scholars disagree about Wesley's relationship to the age in which he lived. Thus, across the years, one group of scholars has read Wesley as a reactionary figure who was determined to turn back the clock to an age in which the majority of people still believed in miracles, demonic possession and divine intervention. A more recent group of scholars read Wesley as a progressive figure who was out ahead of the curve in adapting Christianity to the early modern world. As we will see, what these two ways of reading Wesley have in common is an interpretation of the age in which Wesley lived. Both groups regard eighteenth-century English church and society as increasingly secular.

The third thing that is perplexing about Wesley is the extent to which scholars struggle to discern a unity between Wesley's theological commitments on the one hand, and his ecclesiastical and political commitments on the other. For example, scholars who see in Wesley's political commitments a strong democratic impulse are often at a loss when they are asked to explain the fact that Wesley ran the Methodist societies in an overtly hierarchical fashion. Indeed, very late in his life, Wesley went so far as to say of the Methodists, 'We are no republicans, and never intend to be.'[3] Similarly, scholars who regard Wesley as politically committed to the monarchy – and therefore to hierarchy – often suggest that this was inconsistent with his theological commitment to a doctrine of unlimited atonement. Few, if any, scholars to date have provided an account of Wesley's life and thought in which there is a recognizable unity or coherence between his ecclesiastical, political and theological commitments.

The ultimate aim of this volume is to provide just such an account. In other words, my aim is to provide an account of Wesley that takes him seriously when he says,

> Above all, mark that man who talks of loving the Church, and does not love the King. If he does not love the King, he cannot love God. And if he does not love God, he cannot love the Church. He loves the Church and the King just alike. For indeed he loves neither one nor the other.
>
> O beware, you who truly love the Church, and therefore cannot but love the King; beware of dividing the King and the Church, any more than the King and country. Let others do as they will, what is that to you? Act you as an honest man, a loyal subject, a true Englishman, a lover of the country, a lover of the Church; in one word, a Christian![4]

Showing a unity and coherence among Wesley's ecclesiastical, political and theological commitments will require us to meet head-on the first two perplexities mentioned above. We can not simply provide a few illustrative quotations and then assert that there was a unity and coherence to Wesley's life and thought. After all, what is at issue here is the fact that a great many scholars have suggested that remarks like the one above should not be taken at face value. Thus to make a case for the unity and coherence of Wesley's life and thought will require us, among other things, to peel back the layers of the history of interpretation of Wesley's ecclesiastical, political and theological commitments. With these things in mind, here is how the volume will unfold.

Chapter One consists of a brief biography of Wesley, in which I have deliberately emphasized some of the aspects of Wesley's life that have led scholars to question whether Wesley was really a 'Church of England man' or a High Church Tory. Aside from my criterion for selection, there is nothing especially unique about my telling of the story of Wesley's life. Thus this chapter is primarily for the benefit of readers who have little know-ledge of Wesley's life or for readers who feel they are in need of a refresher. Those who know Wesley's life story well may skip ahead to Chapter Two without any significant loss.

Chapter Two is pivotal for the rest of the book. At the outset, I will review the reasons that scholars doubt whether Wesley was as deeply committed to the Church of England as he claimed (the first perplexity described above). I will then demonstrate that these reasons reflect back-ground assumptions about eighteenth-century English church and soci-ety, assumptions I will refer to collectively as *the secularization thesis*. Next, I will show that, on the secularization thesis, scholars have drawn drastically different conclusions about Wesley (the second perplexity described above). As a way forward, I will provide an alternative reading of eighteenth-century English Church and society. I will refer to this alter-native reading as the *Anglican stabilization thesis*. Finally, I will contend that, in the light of this thesis, Wesley's claim to be a 'Church of England man' appears more credible because, in a confessional state, allegiance to the Church cannot be evaluated primarily on the basis of sensibilities concerning clergy conduct. Rather, it must be evaluated primarily on the basis of the level of commitment exhibited to the aspects of the Church that were deemed most important for the stability and the maintenance of the confessional state. In eighteenth-century England, those aspects were the Trinity and the sacraments, two things to which Wesley was resolutely committed.

For this reading of Wesley's ecclesiastical commitments to hold, Wesley must be shown to have been deeply committed to the other political insti-tutions of the confessional state, namely, divine right monarchy and the constitution. Unfortunately, the majority of scholars today argue that Wesley was much more progressive than that. Indeed, over against Wesley's claims to be a High Church Tory, many scholars insist that he was actu-ally a proto-liberal democrat. Thus I will spend a good deal of Chapter Three assessing these claims. Ultimately, I will conclude that Theodore R. Weber's description of Wesley's politics as a form of Tory constitutional-ism is the most convincing to date. Moreover, I will observe that Weber's portrait of Wesley coheres well with the politics of the confessional state which I have described in Chapter Two. However, I will conclude by not-ing that Weber himself was doubly perplexed by what he perceived to be a deep incoherence between Wesley's politics and his theology.

Chapter Four will provide an account of Wesley's theological commit-ments that, contrary to Weber's perceptions, coheres well with and sup-ports Wesley's ecclesiastical and political commitments. More specifically, I will make the case that there are deep logical similarities between Wesley's covenantal Arminian and economic Trinitarian theology on the one hand, and his Tory constitutionalism on the other. I will also show that, contrary to popular belief, there is no necessary connection between Wesley's doctrine of the unlimited atonement and a democratic impulse in politics. Thus there is no incoherence between Wesley's doctrine of salvation and his rejection of popular sovereignty.

In the conclusion to the volume, I will claim that there is a logical consistency running through Wesley's ecclesiastical, political and theological commitments. However, I will also suggest that there is something deeper than logical consistency here, namely, a robust doctrine of divine providence. Further, I will suggest that, when combined with his covenantal Arminianism, a robust doctrine of providence is what best enables us to discern a unity and a consistency in Wesley's life and thought. It is also what best explains the tensions and apparent inconsistencies, especially the tensions and apparent inconsistencies between his commitment to Methodism and his commitment to the Church of England. More accurately, it enables us to see that the tensions and apparent inconsistencies are among the best witnesses to the unity and consistency of Wesley's life and thought. If we have not noticed this before, then it is likely because the grace to which Wesley thought himself responsible was more comprehensive than we have dared to think or imagine.

Finally, by way of introduction, I should note that this volume is intended for a broad academic audience. I have written it with advanced undergraduate and graduate students in mind, including students interested in the history of the church, politics and theology in eighteenth-century England. In all of these areas, John Wesley is a particularly fascinating figure. What is most fascinating, however, is the way in which church, politics and theology bear constantly on one another in Wesley's life and thought. Thus this book is especially for students who are interested in the political dimensions of theology and church and the theological dimensions of politics as manifested in the life of Wesley, to which we now turn.

CHAPTER ONE

SPREADING THE GOSPEL: METHODISM AND THE EVANGELICAL REVIVAL

At this day the gospel leaven . . . hath so spread in various parts of Europe, particularly in England, Scotland, Ireland, in the islands, in the north and south, from Georgia to New England and Newfoundland, that sinners have been truly converted to God, throughly changed both in heart and in life; not by tens, or by hundreds only, but by thousands, yea, by myriads!
John Wesley, 'The Signs of the Times'

As strange as it may seem by twenty-first-century lights, in order rightly to understand John Wesley, we must begin by taking seriously the fact that he was born to parents who were converts to the Church of England from Puritan nonconformity. For many contemporary readers of Wesley, this may seem like a rather mundane matter. Was a switch from the Puritan to the Anglican Church in the late seventeenth century not like a switch from the Methodist to the Presbyterian Church today? Was it not simply a matter of choosing among Protestant churches with slight differences in theology, worship and polity? No, it was not. A switch from Puritan non-conformity to the established church had significantly more far-reaching consequences.

In some ways, a more apt parallel today might be a switch from Protestantism to Roman Catholicism. Even then, depending on where a person lives, it could be argued that a switch from Puritan nonconformity to the Church of England in the late seventeenth century was still more far-reaching in its consequences. This would be true, for example, if we were comparing the latter switch with, say, a switch from the Baptist Church to the Roman Catholic Church in the United States of America.

What is at stake here? What made the switch from Puritan noncon-formity to the Church of England so significant? To see the significance of this switch, it will help to continue the comparison with a switch from the Baptist to the Roman Catholic Church in America. For all the differences between the Baptist and the Roman Catholic Church, a switch from one to the other would in no way inhibit a person's ability to hold an office in the federal, state and local governments of the United States of America, to attend a public university, or to serve in a branch of the military. Such is life in a liberal democracy. By contrast, a switch from Puritan nonconformity to the Church of England after the Restoration in 1660 was essential if a person wanted to hold a government position, attend Oxford or Cambridge University, earn a living as a minister, or serve in the military. Such was life in a confessional state.

Samuel and Susanna Wesley knew the consequences of a switch from nonconformity to the Church of England as well as anyone. More accurately, they knew the consequences of remaining in nonconformity after the Restoration. Thus Samuel Wesley's grandfather and father were victims of the great ejection of nonconforming clergy in 1662. They were literally thrown out of their churches and homes. And while Susanna Wesley's father, a well-known dissenting preacher in London, did not suffer the same fate, she was surely aware of the political consequences of remaining in dissent.

None of this is to suggest that either Samuel or Susanna joined the Church of England simply to avail themselves of a wider range of career opportunities, as though being a member of the established church guaranteed them a living of any kind. On the contrary, plenty of people who were members of the Church of England in the late seventeenth century lived at the very bottom of the social ladder. Moreover, member of the Church of England or not, Susanna's career prospects were dismal. It was, after all, still very much a man's world.

As things turned out, conversion to the Church of England made it possible for Samuel Wesley to attend Exeter College, Oxford, and ultimately to earn a living as the rector of the Epworth parish. However, conversion from nonconformity to the established church also had its consequences. Thus Samuel was threatened by nonconformist mobs at Epworth, and many believe that the Epworth rectory was set ablaze at least twice by Samuel's nonconformist opponents. In their eyes, Samuel Wesley was a traitor.

Samuel and Susanna's motivations for leaving nonconformity for the established church are probably lost to history. What we do know is that, whatever their motivations, when the Wesleys joined the Church of England, they did so with an enthusiasm and commitment typical of new converts. Put simply, Samuel and Susanna Wesley embraced the full implications of their move, immersing themselves in the Anglican political theology of their day. They wholeheartedly believed that God had ordained both the established church and the King, they readily gave assent to the doctrines of the Trinity and passive obedience and they cherished the means of grace available in the established church, especially the sacraments.

In keeping with these doctrines, Samuel and Susanna also committed themselves to the principle of subordination, according to which society was viewed as arranged by God in an organic and hierarchical fashion. On this principle, the key to a healthy society was the recognition and acceptance of one's place in the order of things. Thus the primary goal of late seventeenth- and eighteenth-century Anglican politics was the establishment and maintenance of order through subordination at all levels of society, from church and state all the way down to family and social organizations. Indeed, the principle of subordination was like a code written into everything from statute law to initiation rites for clerical offices. For example, the consecration of bishops included a prayer for the obedience of the people. Similarly, the ordination rite for priests and deacons included a pledge reverently to obey the Ordinary and any other minister who is given charge over them. For that matter, even bishops had to 'profess and promise all due reverence and obedience to the Archbishop and to the Metropolitan Church'.[1] At the level of the family, the Prayer Book made it clear that wives were to 'obey their husbands'.[2]

From the standpoint of the twentieth century, all of this no doubt sounds strange. From the perspective of those who were committed to the established church in the late seventeenth century, no idea had a stronger pedigree than the idea that a well-ordered society was ordained by God. After all, it was an idea that went at least as far back as Richard Hooker, who once wrote,

> Without order there is no living in public society, because the want thereof is the mother of confusion, whereupon division of necessity followeth, and out of division inevitable destruction . . . And if things or persons be ordered this doth imply that they are distinguished by degrees. For order is a gradual disposition . . . [for] the very Deity itself both keepeth, and requireth for ever this to be kept as law, that whensoever there is a coagmentation of many, the lowest be knit to the highest by that which being interjacent may cause each to cleave unto [the] other, and so all to continue one.[3]

There is no reason to believe that, upon their conversion, Samuel and Susanna Wesley were unaware of the political theology of the established church. Nor is there reason to think that they did not intend to support it wholeheartedly. On the contrary, all the evidence suggests that they took this political theology with its ultimate aim of a well-ordered society with utmost seriousness.

Then again, Samuel and Susanna Wesley had been reared in nonconformity, and from time to time their past caught up with them. This was particularly true for Susanna. Thus, despite her deep loyalty to the Church of England, she did not hesitate to question prevailing sensibilities about the right ordering of things. More specifically, she adhered to the principle of subordination, but she often challenged the application of it.

For example, it is well-known that, as late as 1702, Susanna called into question the legitimacy of the Glorious Revolution, despite the fact that Samuel clearly supported the Hanoverian monarchy.[4] As the story goes, when Susanna refused to say 'Amen' to Samuel's prayers for the King, he confronted her, declaring that they could not share the same bed if they did not share the same King. When Susanna refused to ask forgiveness, Samuel promptly left home for a time. Upon his return, which happened more or less to coincide with the ascension of Anne to the throne, John Wesley was conceived, 'the fruits of reconciliation'.

Similarly, on more than one occasion, Susanna challenged prevailing sensibilities concerning the limits of female lay leadership in giving religious instruction in a parish. For example, when Samuel went away for a time, Susanna took it upon herself to lead parishioners in the study of scripture and in prayer. Upon discovering this, Samuel promptly chastised Susanna for overstepping her bounds. Susanna's response is at once subtle and suggestive, demonstrating that, in early eighteenth-century England, one could conceive not only of subordination among the members of English society, but also of an ultimate form of subordination between each individual member and God. Thus, on the one hand, she made it clear that she was prepared to honour the principle of subordination, telling Samuel that, if he would give her a *'positive command'*, she would follow it.[5] On the other hand, however, Susanna reminded Samuel that, while he could invoke the principle of subordination by forbidding her to give religious instruction in the parish, he would one day have to answer to God for it.

Such was the home into which John Wesley was born on 17 June 1703 (Julian calendar). It was a home in which both parents professed the strongest allegiance to God, to the Church of England, and to the King. Moreover, it was a home in which ready assent was given to the Trinity, to the Christology of the great ecumenical creeds, and to the Thirty-Nine Articles of Religion, and in which the scriptures, prayer, the confession of sin and the sacraments were regarded as instrumental, even essential, to salvation. Finally, it was a home in which a well-ordered society was linked to the principle of subordination, although, as we have just seen, the application of the principle did not go unchallenged.

How much of this rubbed off on John Wesley? To what extent did he follow in his parents' footsteps? As with most children, it is safe to say that some things 'took' more than others. Actually, in Wesley's case, most things took. For example, Wesley was deeply committed to the Trinity, the Christology of the great ecumenical creeds, the Thirty-Nine Articles of Religion and the Book of Common Prayer. Likewise, he was convinced that scripture, prayer, the confession of sin and the sacraments were instrumental, if not essential, to salvation. Moreover, John Wesley clearly believed that the principle of subordination was God-ordained as essential to a well-ordered society. Thus, as we will see, he viewed subordination and order as normative in English church and society, and he emphasized subordination and order in the Methodist societies as well. However, like his mother, he was not unwilling to challenge the application of the principle of subordination. Also like his mother, Wesley would not hesitate to justify his actions by trumping the logic of subordination among members of English church and society with the logic of subordination between individuals, most notably himself, and God. Consequently, many of his contemporaries would suspect him of enthusiasm.[6] Moreover, as we will see, many people, including his own brother, Charles, perceived Wesley was playing too fast and loose with prevailing sensibilities concerning clergy conduct, the limits of the authority of elders, the role of the laity in the church, parish boundaries and the like. As a result, they often suspected him of separatist or nonconformist tendencies. Indeed, many believed that, before he died, Wesley deliberately laid the necessary groundwork for the Methodists to separate from the Church of England.

We will deal with the question of whether Wesley ever intended to separate from the Church of England in the next chapter. For the remainder of this chapter, it will be task enough to provide a sketch of Wesley's life and ministry that highlights both his Anglican commitments and the ways in which he challenged the application of the principle of subordination. It is to that task that we now turn.

THE EARLY YEARS

John Wesley's childhood was as well-ordered and well-disciplined as one could imagine. All told, Wesley spent the first 11 years of his life in the Epworth rectory in Lincolnshire, during which time Susanna Wesley watched over her son's early education and spiritual formation through an intensive homeschooling programme in which Thursdays were devoted especially to John. A stickler for organization and orderliness, Susanna instilled in her children a strong respect and preference for the same. Most importantly, she fostered in John and the other children an early knowledge and love of the scriptures and a strong sense of duty to God, Church and King.

Among the many positive consequences of Susanna's insistence on order and discipline may be included the fact that John went on to thrive academically as a student at Charterhouse school, where he attended from 1714 to 1720, and ultimately at Christ Church, Oxford, from which he graduated in 1724. However, there may also have been a few negative consequences, particularly in John's case. Predisposed to seriousness, the rigidity of Susanna's methods may have contributed to John's lack of a sense of humour and inflexibility later in life.

One additional aspect of life in the Epworth parish is especially worth noting. If John inherited a penchant for orderliness and discipline from his mother, then he inherited from his father an interest in the role of religious societies in the spiritual and moral renewal of English church and society.[7] A corresponding member of the Society for Promoting Christian Knowledge in London, Samuel Wesley established a religious society in the Epworth parish devoted to the reading of scripture and other theological materials, mutual confession and prayer, strong moral discipline and the pursuit of holiness. On the one hand, it is impossible to know how much such things actually influenced John. On the other hand, when we consider that John Wesley spent the majority of his life organizing and leading religious societies, it is hard to believe that Samuel's involvement in the work of the societies was not a source of inspiration for his son.

THE OXFORD YEARS

After several years at Charterhouse, Wesley began studies at Christ Church, Oxford in 1720. In Wesley's day, Oxford was 'something of a glorified high school crossed with a finishing school for grandees'. Nonetheless, he managed to gain 'a priceless education', thanks in part to the organization and discipline he inherited from his mother.[8] Among other things, Wesley proved himself an avid reader during this time, taking a special interest in Jeremy Taylor's *Rules and Exercises of Holy Living and Holy Dying*, as well as classic works of medieval spirituality, most notably Thomas a Kempis' *The Imitation of Christ*. Through these and other works, Wesley became more convinced than ever of the importance of a well-ordered and well-disciplined life, as well as the need to be fully subordinate to God.

It was also during his student days at Oxford that Wesley weighed carefully the importance of order and subordination in the church. Thus when it came time to consider ordination, Wesley weighed the matter most carefully. Among other things, he wanted to be sure that he could truly be subordinate to the Anglican standards of doctrine as enshrined in the Thirty-Nine Articles of Religion. Consequently, Wesley took the time to think his way through some theological sticking points before seeking ordination.

In 1724, after careful deliberation, Wesley officially entered the ministry of the Church of England when Bishop John Potter ordained him a deacon. On 17 March 1726, Wesley was elected a Fellow of Lincoln College, and two years later, Bishop Potter ordained him an elder. As we have seen, Wesley's ordinations would have included a pledge to be subordinate to those over him. Interestingly enough, he made good on this pledge the first time that he had the opportunity to do so. Having left Oxford for a stint in parish ministry, Wesley promptly returned when the rector of Lincoln College requested that he resume his duties as a Fellow. Of course, it did not hurt that Wesley thoroughly enjoyed what he once called 'the groves of academe'. Nonetheless, the fact remains that Wesley did return when he was asked to do so.

Upon returning to Oxford in the spring of 1729, Wesley discovered that his brother Charles and a few others had begun to devote themselves to the study of scripture, church attendance, prayer and mutual confession of sin, and to helping people in need. In effect, he discovered the makings of a religious society. Almost immediately, Wesley joined the group, and before long he was recognized by outsiders as the group's chief leader. Suffice it to say, the recognition was not something to be coveted. Unsure what to make of Wesley and his cohorts, among whom was a young George Whitefield, a number of people began referring to them rather derisively as the Holy Club, the Bible Moths, the Sacramentarians and the Methodists. For better or worse, the name 'Methodists' eventually stuck.

Despite the ridicule, Wesley and his little band of Methodists continued to study scripture, partake of the sacraments, attend worship, honour the fast days of the ancient church, visit those in prison and help the poor. In addition to his duties as a tutor, Wesley began to focus his time and energies on what would become one of the hallmarks of his life and ministry, namely, sermon writing and preaching. Thus, following his return from parish ministry at Epworth and Wroot in 1729, he began preaching frequently in nearby churches and prisons. Moreover, he soon became one of the more popular preachers in Christ Church Cathedral and St Mary's at Oxford. And while most scholars agree that the sermons Wesley wrote during his Oxford days are generally unmemorable, there is also a near consensus that the second sermon that he preached before the University, 'The Circumcision of the Heart' (1733), was among the best that he would ever write.

Depending on one's perspective, a final episode during Wesley's Oxford years might be viewed as the first sign that Wesley would one day challenge the application of the principle of subordination. Thus, in 1734, with his health now failing, Samuel Wesley invited John to take over for him as the pastor of the Epworth parish. In a decision that was somewhat alarming to his family, John declined the invitation, saying that he believed his services were needed more at Oxford than at Epworth. To be sure, the refusal did not break any ecclesiastical laws. However, it clearly stretched the boundaries of what Wesley's own family regarded as proper clergy conduct, not to mention sensibilities concerning the subordination of children to their parents.

THE SAVANNAH YEARS

For having made such a fuss about the great need for his services at Oxford, Wesley failed to make good on his decision to remain there. Shortly after declining his father's invitation to take over his parish, Wesley and several of the Oxford Methodists, including his brother Charles, joined a missionary expedition to Savannah, Georgia. According to Wesley, he was struggling with his faith, and he hoped that the trip would somehow help him to overcome his growing fears and doubts concerning the state of his own soul. In many respects, it had exactly the opposite effect. As the story goes, Wesley had a terrifying encounter with a storm while on his way across the Atlantic Ocean. During this storm, he feared that he would die. To his astonishment, a group of Moravians on board the ship quietly sang songs through the whole ordeal. On the one hand, Wesley was deeply impressed by their faith. On the other hand, he was now even more convinced of his own lack of faith.

Following the storm, Wesley sought advice from the Moravians. Among other things, he wanted to know how they were able to remain calm during such a violent storm. A Moravian by the name of August Spangenberg responded by putting a series of questions to Wesley. In short, the Moravian wanted to know whether Wesley had experienced the witness of the Holy Spirit that he was a child of God. This question must have hit especially hard given that, only a few months earlier, Wesley's own father, while dying, had urged Wesley to remember the inner witness of the Holy Spirit. When Wesley dodged the question, Spangenberg inquired as to whether Wesley knew Jesus Christ as his saviour. Once again, Wesley was unsure how to answer. If anything, the conversation seems to have added to Wesley's fear that he was not a person of genuine faith.

In the final analysis, Wesley's time as a missionary was a failure. In addition to failing to overcome his fears and doubts, Wesley's attempt to impose a well-ordered and highly disciplined approach to religion did not go over well in the new world. To top things off, Wesley failed miserably at romantic love while in Savannah. Tired of waiting on him to make up his mind, Sophia Hopkey, in all likelihood the love of Wesley's life, was given in marriage to a rival suitor. Wesley responded by barring her from the sacraments, an act which landed him before a jury for clergy misconduct. And while it was arguable that he had not broken any laws, he had clearly offended the sensibilities of some important individuals in the colony. One might say that he had violated the logic of subordination by abusing his power over a lay person. Knowing that the jury was not likely to reach a favourable verdict on his behalf, Wesley fled Savannah in the middle of the night. It was December 1737. After 22 months abroad, he was on his way back home.

THE FETTER LANE YEARS

Almost immediately upon his return from America, Wesley met a Moravian minister named Peter Böhler. In many ways, it was a relationship that changed Wesley's life. Initially, Wesley consulted with Böhler about the nature of faith. By this time, Wesley had decided that he had faith but that his faith was not yet strong enough to conquer the fear of death. Böhler disagreed, and he eventually convinced Wesley that he lacked faith altogether. For Böhler, faith was a zero-sum game. One either had it entirely, or one did not have it at all.

Wesley was now so convinced that he lacked faith, he decided that he should quit preaching. Once again, Böhler disagreed, saying, 'Preach faith *till* you have it, and then, *because* you have it, you *will* preach faith.'[9] Wesley followed Böhler's advice, preaching repeatedly in the days and months ahead on salvation by faith. Indeed, Wesley preached so enthusiastically during this time that he was barred from a number of churches.

In addition to preaching on salvation by faith in prisons and churches, Wesley began visiting and preaching at a number of religious societies in and around Oxford and London. Among these was a loosely organized group meeting at the home of James Hutton. On 1 May 1738, Böhler met with Hutton and Wesley, organizing what would soon become known as the Fetter Lane Society.

Mere days after the establishment of the new society at Fetter Lane, two things happened that had a significant impact on Wesley. First, Böhler left for America, entrusting the leadership of the Fetter Lane Society to Wesley. Second, on Whitsunday, Wesley's younger brother Charles had a profound experience of the inner witness of the Holy Spirit assuring him of his salvation.

Hearing about Charles' newfound assurance sent Wesley into another tailspin. All the old doubts about whether he really had faith re-surfaced with a vengeance. Fortunately, three days later, while attending a religious society meeting at Aldersgate Street, Wesley experienced for himself the assurance of salvation for which he had been longing. Here is Wesley's well-known account of the event:

> In the evening I went very unwillingly to a society in Aldersgate Street, where one was reading Luther's Preface to the Epistle to the Romans. About a quarter before nine, while he was describing the change which God works in the heart through faith in Christ, I felt my heart strangely warmed. I felt I did trust in Christ, Christ alone for salvation, and an assurance was given me that he had taken away *my* sins, even *mine*, and saved *me* from the law of sin and death.[10]

For better or worse, Wesley is best known in many quarters today for the simple phrase 'I felt my heart strangely warmed.' Indeed, people who know almost nothing else about Wesley are sometimes familiar with this little phrase.[11] Interestingly enough, Wesley himself did not dwell for long on the sensation that he felt in his heart that night. Consequently, over-emphasis on this phrase often distracts attention from what happened next.

Despite the fuss made today over his Aldersgate conversion experience, the fact is that Aldersgate did not put an end to Wesley's struggles with faith and assurance.[12] The reason for this is simple enough. In addition to teaching him that salvation was by faith, the Moravians also taught Wesley that, when he truly came to faith, a noticeable increase in the fruits of the Spirit would soon follow. Thus, in the days following the meeting at Aldersgate, Wesley was once again taking his spiritual temperature. Unfortunately, while he had a strong sense of peace, the other fruits of the Spirit, most notably joy, did not appear to be on the increase, which caused Wesley to continue to question whether or not he had true faith.

Determined to resolve his worries, Wesley once again sought the advice of the Moravians. This time, however, he decided to go to the very source of Moravianism, namely, Germany. Though he had no way of knowing it at the time, this would prove to be one of the most important trips Wesley would take.

Soon after he arrived at the Moravian community at Herrnhut, Wesley discovered that there was a significant difference between German and English Moravianism. More specifically, Wesley noticed that Nicholas von Zinzendorf, the leader of the community at Herrnhutt, differed from Peter Böhler in his understanding of the doctrine of salvation by faith. Whereas Böhler had insisted that upon coming to faith a person would have full assurance of salvation and a sudden increase in the fruits of the Spirit, Zinzendorf maintained that justification by faith could precede both full assurance and the fruits of the Spirit. In other words, Zinzendorf distinguished more carefully between the specific doctrine of justification by faith and the wider network of doctrines related to salvation, including assurance and sanctification. Given the number of years Wesley had been struggling with these issues, the distinction proved a Godsend.

When Wesley finally returned home to England in the fall of 1738, he discovered that the Fetter Lane Society had grown considerably in his absence. Over the next few months, he continued to mull over what he had learned from the German Moravians, ultimately embracing the distinction between faith and assurance. He even added his own twist on the subject, distinguishing between the assurance of faith and the assurance of salvation, the latter having to do with the doctrine of perseverance.

These distinctions did not sit well with some of the members of the Fetter Lane Society. Consequently, Wesley suddenly found himself at odds with the Society. In addition to theological differences, Wesley was concerned that, under the influence of the new Moravian leader, Philipp Heinrich Molther, the Society had ceased attending to the means of grace. Insisting that their only need was Christ himself, Molther taught that people should forego the means of grace and simply remain still, waiting for salvation. Wesley disagreed strongly. For all his time with the Moravians, he remained deeply Anglican in his belief that the means of grace, most notably the sacraments, were instrumental, even essential, to salvation.

In 1740, Wesley parted ways with the Fetter Lane Society. This depart-ure was no doubt made easier by the fact that Wesley now had a number of other irons in the fire, not the least of which was his involvement in another newly formed society in London. Most scholars agree that this was a major turning point in Wesley's life. Indeed, at least one scholar has argued that Wesley's departure from Fetter Lane for this new society constitutes the 'commencement' of Methodism.[13] Whatever we make of this claim, it is important to locate Methodism within a wider horizon. It was not sim-ply that Wesley switched societies at this time. Also important was the fact that, while Wesley's relationship with the Fetter Lane Society was crumbling, his relationship with George Whitefield and what would soon be known as the revival was beginning to take off. Indeed, thanks largely to Whitefield, the revival was already well underway.

THE REVIVAL: THE EARLY YEARS

As we have seen, Wesley spent a great deal of time in the 1730s checking his own spiritual temperature. He had looked high and low for a resolution to his worries over faith and assurance of salvation. He had literally sailed across an ocean two times, and he had spent years discoursing with the Moravians in an attempt to sort out his personal doubts in this area.

Beginning in the fall of 1738, two things happened that helped to redir-ect Wesley's time and energy toward something other than the state of his own soul. First, Wesley rediscovered the theological riches of his own Anglican tradition, most notably, the *Book of Homilies*. As things turned out, Wesley's hard-won understanding of the relationship between faith and assurance was virtually identical to what he found there. The irony was that Wesley had gone half way around the world in search of what had been readily available to him in his own theological backyard. The discov-ery must have been a sobering one.

Second, Wesley realized that, while he was busy trying to convince him-self that he was really a Christian, there were amazing things happening all around him. In the fall of 1738, he read Jonathan Edwards' eye-opening account of the revival taking place in America, and by the spring of the following year, he was increasingly aware that something similar was hap-pening in England. Whitefield had taken to preaching in the streets, and he was urging Wesley to come to Bristol to see what was happening.

Before we journey with Wesley to Bristol, a word of caution is in order. It is tempting to think that Wesley's participation in the revival marks the beginning of his separation from the Church of England. At one level, this is understandable enough. After all, Whitefield had taken to the streets and the countryside because, like Wesley, he had been barred from a number of pulpits in the city. The point to remember, however, is that the barring of Whitefield and Wesley from pulpits was largely a natural reaction to the fact that they were stretching Anglican sensibilities and boundaries concerning norms for clergy life. Generally speaking, clergy were supposed to do one of two things. They were to take up an academic post, or they were to settle into parish life. That Wesley remained deeply committed to the Church of England is evident in part by his willingness to respond often and at length to those who criticized his refusal to remain in one location. Indeed, it was precisely in responding to criticism that he was violating parish boundaries that Wesley quipped, 'I look upon *all the world* as *my parish*.'[14]

Another point to remember is that much of the uproar over the Methodists at this time was due to the extravagant nature of Whitefield's personality and preaching. For that matter, Whitefield's tactics were stretching Wesley's Anglican sensibilities concerning proper clergy conduct. Thus Wesley admitted that he had a hard time reconciling himself 'to this strange way of preaching in the fields'.[15] Moreover, there is no evidence that Wesley understood his own work as being in any way unrelated to the Church of England. Thus Richard P. Heitzenrater is exactly right when he says that Wesley's role in the revival was to help 'consolidate the work of the Methodists and Moravians within the structures provided by the Church of England'.[16] Finally, it should be noted that those structures prohibited neither religious societies nor outdoor preaching. The revival may have challenged Anglican sensibilities about what was decent and respectable in the way of clergy conduct, but it did not break any ecclesiastical laws.

Despite being initially put off by the spectacle of field-preaching, Wesley preached his first sermon outdoors just a few days after he arrived in Bristol. In the months and years that lay ahead, he would go to preach in a number of outdoor settings, including market places, coal mines, and in graveyards atop tombstones. By Wesley's own account, these activities were 'vile'. In other words, he was well-aware that he was stretching the boundaries of Anglican sensibilities concerning appropriate clergy conduct.

Of course, the most extraordinary thing about field preaching was the crowds. Tens of thousands showed up, many of whom were a part of the working class in and around Bristol. Behind the scenes, however, Wesley remained deeply committed to the work of the religious societies. Thus he frequently visited the existing societies in the area, and he worked to organize new societies. And while attendance at the societies was much smaller than at the open-air preaching events, it can be argued that, far more than field preaching, it was the slow, on-the-ground work of the societies that secured the long-term success of the revival and of Methodism.

While Wesley did his share of field preaching, it was Whitefield who truly excelled in this aspect of the revival. By contrast, Wesley proved especially innovative and holistic in his approach to organizing and equipping the societies. For example, when societies got too big for the private homes in which they originated, Wesley raised money to erect buildings large enough to accommodate the crowds, the most notable of which being the so-called New Room at Bristol. At the same time, he was keenly aware that larger crowds sometimes entailed a loss of personal accountability. Thus he began encouraging his followers voluntarily to join one another in small 'bands' of five or six people for mutual confession and prayer. Finally, as he had done at Oxford, Wesley began to put into place structures and practices designed specifically to help the poor, including the establishment of the Kingswood school for impoverished children.

When Wesley returned to London in the winter of 1739, he helped a group of people restore an old Foundery building for preaching and for society meetings. By spring of the following the year, just as he was putting an end to his relationship with the Fetter Lane Society, a new society began to meet at the recently renovated building. Almost immediately, Wesley began implementing in London the kinds of structures and practices he had just finished putting into place in Bristol, namely, daily preaching times, bands for mutual scripture reading and prayer, collections for the poor and the like.

At this stage, a problem began to emerge that would haunt Wesley for the remainder of his life. There were too many societies spread out between Oxford, London and Bristol and too few preachers to go around. In an effort to meet this challenge, Wesley began authorizing laypersons in the bands and societies to provide leadership in the absence of an ordained elder, a move that soon led to the controversial practice of 'lay preaching'. While lay-preaching did not break any ecclesiastical laws, it clearly stretched perceived boundaries concerning the limits of lay participation in the work of ministry. Of more immediate concern to Wesley, however, was the fact that the appointment of lay leaders was not proving to be enough. As it had with the preachers, the explosive growth of the societies was outpacing the number of qualified lay leaders, making pastoral oversight a continual problem. In response, Wesley introduced a new middle-management structure into the societies known simply as 'classes'. By dividing up the societies into classes based on the geographical proximity of members' residences, he put into place a sophisticated mechanism not only for pastoral oversight but for the collection of money for the poor as well. Wesley was proving himself an organizational genius.

In the midst of all of this, Wesley was increasingly at odds with Whitefield. At the heart of the problem was a sharp disagreement over the doctrines of double predestination and the final perseverance of the elect. In short, Whitefield advocated for, and Wesley opposed, both. Whitefield also opposed Wesley's doctrine of Christian perfection, according to which Christians could be entirely free from sin. When the dispute became public knowledge, Wesley and Whitefield were called to account by the Bishop of London. Once again, Wesley proved more than willing to subject himself to a representative of the Church of England. As things turn out, the Bishop was satisfied with Wesley's explanation, reportedly encouraging Wesley to preach his doctrine of Christian perfection to the entire world.

Needless to say, Wesley was not able to gain such an endorsement from Whitefield, nor Whitefield from Wesley. In the end, the feud resulted in a splitting of the revival into Wesleyan and Calvinist branches. On the Calvinist side, Whitefield enjoyed the patronage of the Countess of Huntingdon, who helped to organize an association of Calvinist preachers into which some of the leaders of the societies associated with Wesley would soon defect. While Whitefield and Wesley remained at odds with one another theologically in the coming decades, they clearly regarded one another as co-labourers in the revival. Thus, when Whitefield died, those in charge of his estate thought it both natural and appropriate to invite Wesley to preach at his funeral. Wesley graciously accepted the invitation, delivering a funeral oration worthy of a saint.

As the societies continued to increase in attendance, the percentage of people from the working or artisan classes and of poor people increased as well. In response to this development, Wesley insisted that the societies' well-to-do members care for the poor among them, and he often found creative ways to help the poor earn income. This belies the myth that the revival was exclusively about connecting people to God. For Wesley, it was also about connecting people with one another.

Due in part to the growth of the societies and in part to the shift in meeting location from private homes to more public buildings, Wesley soon found himself facing accusations that the Methodists were separatists. Indeed, a few people were claiming that, unless the Methodists registered as dissenters, the New Room and the Foundry were illegal meetinghouses. In response to these objections, some of which were registered by members of the Episcopal bench, Wesley patiently and persistently maintained that both he and the Methodists were loyal to the Church of England. Indeed, Wesley sometimes went so far as to argue that the Methodists were considerably more loyal to the Church of England than most.

Occasionally, in the midst of the arguments, Wesley appealed to the logic of subordination to God. Put simply, Wesley was doing the work God called him to do. Ultimately, therefore, he had to answer to God. Unfortunately, in making this move, he invited and subsequently had to respond to charges of enthusiasm. Given the widespread disdain for enthusiasm, Wesley would have been better off sticking with a combination of appeals to ecclesiastical law, to the Methodists' track record of loyalty to the Church of England, and to the fact that no one had given him a direct order either to register the Methodists as dissenters or to close the preaching-houses.

Amid his many responses to his critics, Wesley was now travelling more and more extensively on behalf of the revival, making frequent trips to

Yorkshire, Cornwall, the Midlands, Newcastle, Leicester, Ireland and Wales.[17] The revival may have fragmented into Moravian, Calvinist and Methodist constituencies, but there was still plenty of work to be done. Thus, in 1743, in an effort better to organize and consolidate the societies affiliated with him, Wesley drew up a standardized list of rules for membership. According to this list, those who would remain members of the societies were to avoid doing harm, to do as much good as possible, and faithfully to attend to the ordinances of God. Similarly, in 1744, Wesley called a conference in which he had two big goals. First, he hoped to standardize the teaching and practices of the preachers and leaders in the societies. Second, he wanted to take one more crack at reuniting the Moravian, Calvinist and Methodist branches of the revival. With regard to the latter goal, the conference was a failure. With regard to the former, however, the conference was a success, extending considerably the life of the Methodist branch of the revival.

THE REVIVAL: THE MIDDLE YEARS

From 1738 to 1744, the revival had been by turns astonishing and disappointing. On the one hand, Whitefield, Wesley, Böhler and the others had seen crowds in both the outdoor settings and in the societies that they could never have imagined. Nor could they have predicted the stunning increase in the number of the societies. On the other hand, they were all disappointed by the division and disunity that had set in among them.

After 1744, despite their mutual disappointment, few thought the prospects for reunion likely. Thus Wesley's efforts to streamline the teaching and practices of the Methodist societies at the conference proved the next best thing. Without saying so explicitly, he was attempting to cut his losses and to figure out who was really with him. Thus while Wesley began the conference by insisting on open debates, he was clearly not prepared to lose any of them. By the end of the conference, virtually all of Wesley's positions were affirmed, including his hard won views on faith and assurance, his doctrine of sanctification and his rules for membership and discipline in the societies.

Both the purpose and the effect of the conference was the creation of a sense of connection or togetherness among the societies associated with Wesley. To insure that the sense of connection would last, Wesley took the shrewd step of calling for annual meetings. In doing so, he risked more criticism that he had separatist intentions. Knowing this, he took steps to demonstrate that the Methodists were committed to the Church of England, including admonishing the preachers to do their work as quietly as possible. This good faith effort notwithstanding, accusations of separatism and dissent would not go away. On the contrary, the very next year saw the Methodists accused of Jacobitism in connection with the '45 Rebellion.[18]

For his part, Wesley was able to draw on the Anglican tradition itself to defend the revival. Thus he maintained that Anglican polity had always featured a healthy measure of flexibility. Moreover, the Church of England had both allowed for and benefited from creativity and innovation across the generations. From Wesley's point of view, the revival was simply a renewal movement in the Church of England. If given sufficient space to operate, he was sure that the Methodist movement would be of great benefit to English church and society alike.

Throughout the middle years of the revival, Wesley continued to select and equip lay preachers for the societies. He also kept up a rigorous preaching schedule, and he insisted that the societies and their leaders minister to all the needs of the people. In his preaching during this time, Wesley continued to emphasize repentance for sin, justification by faith, assurance, works of mercy and love, active participation in the means of grace and Christian perfection. In all these respects, the middle years of the revival were a more focused and better organized extension of the work that Wesley had been doing from the beginning.

Among the more distinctive features of the middle years of the revival was Wesley's increased commitment to the publication of works of practical divinity. To be sure, he had been publishing sermons and other apologetic works for several years, but his commitment to this aspect of the revival was now stronger than ever. There were at least two reasons for this. First, there was the now almost constant need to respond to speculation about and criticism of the Methodist societies. Thus, in the 1740s alone, Wesley wrote dozens of tracts, half a dozen major essays, and participated in a lengthy exchange of letters with a critic by the name of 'John Smith', all in an effort to defend the Methodists from charges of popery, Jacobitism, enthusiasm, separation and congregationalism. In virtually all of these writings, Wesley reiterated time and again his own loyalty and that of the Methodists to the Church of England. Similarly, he often pointed out that he was willing to subject himself to express commands of those over him. In Wesley's mind, there was a clear and important distinction between doing things that challenged prevailing sensibilities concerning the right application of the principle of subordination and rejecting the principle of subordination in itself. He may have been guilty of the former, but he was not guilty of the latter.

Second, there was the ever present need to provide materials to help the lay preachers and other leaders of the societies. Together with his younger brother Charles, Wesley published original sermons, hymns, and other devotional and catechetical materials, as well as excerpts from important works of Christian theology and spirituality across the centuries. The most significant of the original works was a three-volume work called *Sermons on Several Occasions*. Published between 1746 and 1750, this collection of Wesley's sermons was meant to provide theological instruction for the preachers. Of the extracts and abridgements that Wesley published during this time, *A Christian Library* was far and away the most important, consisting as it did of some fifty volumes arranged chronologically from the writings of the early church forward. In a closely related move, Wesley also stocked the preaching houses with libraries of books, ranging from works of practical divinity and Christian spirituality to works of poetry, natural philosophy and astronomy.

While Wesley was working to educate the preachers and other leaders of the societies, the societies themselves kept multiplying so that, by 1746, it was proving almost impossible for the preachers to make the rounds. Once again, Wesley's organizational instincts came to the fore. In what was perhaps a desperate move, Wesley divided up the societies into seven preaching circuits, assigning the preachers to monthly rotations among the circuits. This insured that every society would benefit from preaching on a regular basis. Thus out of necessity Wesley committed the preachers to the principle of itinerancy for which Methodists are known to this day.

In addition to insuring that the preachers made the rounds to all the societies, one of Wesley's constant challenges in managing the revival was monitoring the preachers themselves. From the beginning, the revival had attracted its share of quacks claiming to be preachers, and many of the lay preachers lacked formal theological training. However, there were some problems that education could not fix, most notably habitual immoral conduct and a complete lack of the requisite gifts and graces needed for preaching. To weed out these problems, Wesley had begun occasionally examining the preachers as early as 1746. By 1750, things were sufficiently bad that, together with his brother Charles, Wesley undertook to examine all the preachers on an annual basis. Unfortunately, the Wesley brothers disagreed with one another over just how rigorous the examinations should be, John preferring a more lenient and gracious approach, Charles a more thorough and unyielding one. In the end, numerous preachers were expelled from the connection, and a few added to take their places.

The dispute between John and Charles over the examination of the preachers marked the beginning of a rocky period in their relationship. For one thing, Charles was increasingly concerned about the extent to which Wesley's activities were sending separatist signals. Thus he insisted that the preachers, including himself and John, sign an annual covenant not to break with the Church of England.

Aggravating the situation considerably was the fact that, in the 1750s, some of the preachers began to urge Wesley to allow them to administer the sacraments. In 1754, the matter came to a head when Charles informed John that some of the preachers were now taking it upon themselves to administer the sacrament. John responded by insinuating that these preachers were essentially ordained, having been commissioned by John himself to preach the Gospel. His answer did not set well with Charles.

In fact, it made the situation worse, for if John believed that his commissioning people to preach was tantamount to ordination, then he clearly had no regard for order or for the standard application of the principle of subordination with regard to clerical authority. As far as Charles was concerned, such disregard for order was tantamount to separation.

After a great deal of pressure from Charles, John addressed the matter of separation directly and publicly. At the Leeds Conference in 1755, John presented a treatise called 'Ought We to Separate from the Church of England?' The very fact that he had to go out of his way to address the matter at the conference suggests that there was now a vocal minority among the preachers who wanted to entertain the possibility of separation. In the treatise itself, John made it very clear that the Methodists would not separate. He also insisted that un-ordained Methodist preachers were under no circumstances to administer the sacraments. However, neither the treatise nor the signing of yet another covenant not to separate put an end to the matter. Indeed, from this point forward, Wesley would have constantly to deal with requests for permission to administer the sacraments or even to separate from within the movement, as well as with accusations of separation from without. Moreover, as we will see, this would not be the last time that he would get an earful from Charles.

As if the tensions over the administration of the sacraments and the spectre of separation were not enough, the 1760s saw a new round of theological dispute within the Methodist ranks. This time the issue had to do with the doctrine of Christian perfection. When a growing number of Methodists began to claim that they had been made perfect, some of the preachers got carried away. In an effort to emphasize the importance of perfection, they began to teach and preach that perfection was necessary for salvation. Others began preaching that the end of the world was coming soon, urging people to seek perfection while they still had time to do so. Moreover, some preachers insisted that perfection was permanent. Once a person was perfected, they would never sin again. In the most extreme cases, preachers were suggesting that perfection meant not only complete freedom from sin, but immunity from temptation, making them superior to the Lord Jesus Christ himself.

In response to the controversy over perfection and to requests from some of the members of the societies that he set the record straight, Wesley determined that the societies and the preachers needed standards of doctrine. Accordingly, Wesley inserted statements into the Model Deed (the deed for the preaching houses) that restricted the pulpits to people approved by Wesley and preaching in the pulpits to the doctrinal parameters contained in two works, namely, Wesley's *Notes Upon the New Testament* and the now four-volume collection of Wesley's *Sermons*. In doing so, Wesley once again seemed to be sending signals that he was preparing for separation from the Church of England. A more natural reading of this action, however, is to see Wesley as providing a set of standards that spoke to the specific issues over which the societies so often fell into dispute. The standards of doctrine of the Church of England simply did not speak directly to the doctrine of Christian perfection or to the specifics of the debates *within* and *among* the societies over predestination, assurance and the like.

There can be no doubt that Wesley was aware that people might read the adoption of doctrinal standards as preparation for separation. Thus, in addition to supplementing the Anglican standards of doctrine with the *Notes Upon the New Testament* and the *Sermons*, he also incorporated into the *Minutes* of that year's conference a set of admonishments concerning the Methodists' manner of relating to the Church of England. Wesley was now performing an ecclesiastical version of a high-wire act. On the one hand, he was trying to care for and guide the Methodist societies and the wider revival of which they were a part. On the other hand, he was continuing to insist that Methodism was a renewal movement *within* the Church of England and, as such, that relations with the established church were non-negotiable. The seriousness with which Wesley took this relationship is evident in the list of admonishments, which reads as follows:

(1) Let all our Preachers go to church. (2) Let all our people go constantly. (3) Receive the sacrament at every opportunity. (4) Warn all against niceness in hearing, a great and prevailing evil. (5) Warn them likewise against despising the prayers of the Church. (6) Against calling our Society a Church, or the Church. (7) Against calling our Preachers Ministers, our houses meeting-houses (call them plain preaching-houses). (9) Do not license them as such.[19]

Having provided the preachers and societies with doctrinal standards and with explicit norms for their relationship to the Church of England, Wesley spent much of his remaining time in the 1760s writing and publishing sermons containing advice on practical and ethical matters. He advised them on how to handle their money, on how to dress and on the nature and limits of friendship. In all of these areas, Wesley proved himself particularly aware both of the diversity of class represented in the societies, as well as the growing affluence of many of the Methodists. Thus, as the long middle years of the revival drew to a close, Wesley continued his practice of giving holistic advice to those under his supervision and care. Far from only worrying about their souls (a popular stereotype of Wesley), he cared deeply about their minds, bodies and social interactions as well.

THE REVIVAL: THE LATER YEARS

At this stage, it should be said that there are no clear lines of demarcation between the early, middle and later years of the revival. Indeed, we can readily recognize a large cluster of activities that recur throughout Wesley's life and ministry. Thus, beginning as early as the Oxford years and continuing well into old age, Wesley worked tirelessly to come to terms with a network of theological issues in and around the doctrine of salvation, to respond to critics of his theological positions and of the revival itself, to manage and resolve internal disputes within the societies, to develop and deploy new strategies to deal with the growth of the societies, to write and to publish materials to aid in the education and work of the preachers, to collect and to dispense money for the needy, to erect new preaching-houses, to oversee the annual conferences, and to give guidance to the societies' members on issues ranging from theology to health care and personal finance.

Nevertheless, it is possible to envision the revival in terms of early, middle and later years based on a few major themes. For example, the early years are characterized by the need to sort through the chaos and confusion generated by people with different theological perspectives operating in the same space toward similar ends. The middle years, by contrast, have to do with the separation into more or less distinct groups (Moravian, Methodist and Calvinist), the consolidation of theology and ministry within those groups, the failed negotiation of relations between the various groups and the ongoing negotiation of relations between individual groups and the established church.

By almost all accounts, the later years of the revival had two distinguishing features. On the one hand, there was the sudden re-emergence of America in the overall equation. On the other hand, there was the need to make provisions for leadership of the societies after Wesley's death. Thus it is with these two major issues that we will be concerned from this point forward.

In one sense, there were always connections between the revival and the American colonies. For example, Whitefield was among a number of people who spent a great deal of time in America. Yet from the late 1760s on, Wesley found his attention increasingly divided between the work that needed to be done at home and the quickening pace of the work abroad.

Having said this, the first thing to note about the spread of Methodism in America is that neither Wesley nor Francis Asbury was instrumental in the very beginning. To be sure, Wesley had been to America in the 1730s, and Asbury was later to become one of the first bishops of American Methodism. However, as we have seen, Wesley had virtually no success in America, and Asbury was only in his first year of service as a Methodist preacher in England when Wesley began receiving requests for preachers in 1768 from people already on the ground. Among those asking for help was the Irish Methodist local preacher Philip Embury in New York, and some people associated with another Irish Methodist preacher in Maryland by the name of Robert Strawbridge.

That it was the Irish who helped launch the first Methodist classes in America is not particularly surprising. After all, Wesley had spent a great deal of time and energy personally overseeing the revival in Ireland. All told, he made more than forty trips to Ireland, spending a total of more than five years of his life there. Thus he must have been more than a little pleased when he discovered that a couple of Irish Methodist preachers were working to start societies in America.

Whatever Wesley may have felt about the Irish Methodists' efforts to start societies in America, he was initially unable to answer their requests for help. When he took the requests to the preachers at the annual conference in 1768, they concluded that they simply did not have anyone to spare for the upstart societies in America. The matter clearly weighed on Wesley's mind. Thus, in the following year, he brought the request once again before the conference. This time, the preachers voted to send Richard Boardman and Joseph Pilmore to New York and Philadelphia respectively. Two years later, the conference voted to send Richard Wright and Francis Asbury as well. Asbury was only 26 years old when he arrived in the new world, having a grand total of four years' ministerial experience under his belt.

Suffice it to say, the request for preachers was not the only reason that America was on Wesley's mind. Indeed, one of the striking features of the later years of the revival is the dramatic increase in Wesley's political writings, the majority of which have to do either directly or indirectly with the American quest for liberty, the war for American Independence and the slave trade. From 1768 to 1782, Wesley published no less than a dozen political essays, through which he demonstrated his commitment to the doctrine of subordination with respect to the King.[20]

During this time, Wesley strongly opposed the American quest for liberty and independence. Interestingly enough, one of his objections was that a cry for liberty by a people who enslaved other people was disingenuous from the start. However, more was at stake than Wesley's judgement that the Americans were hypocritical. Wesley's opposition to the American cause was creating problems for the fledgling Methodist societies in America. As a result of their association with Wesley, the earliest American Methodists were increasingly perceived as loyalists and therefore as a threat to the quest for independence. By the time the war ended, the Methodist societies in America would lose approximately half their members, and all but one of the preachers still in connection with Wesley would return home, Asbury being the exception.

Also interesting is the fact that, after publishing the anti-slavery essay 'Thoughts Upon Slavery' in 1774, Wesley seems to have turned his attention to other matters. Thus he had little else to say about slavery for more than a decade. When he finally returned to the issue in 1787, he did so with a firm resolve, throwing his considerable weight behind the newly formed

Society for the Abolition of the Slave Trade and re-publishing his essay from 1774. In the following year, Wesley included a considerable amount of anti-slavery materials in the *Arminian Magazine*, now the official periodical of Methodism. Most importantly, mere days before his death, Wesley wrote an impassioned letter to a young William Wilberforce, admonishing him to keep up his campaign against 'that execrable villainy, which is the scandal of religion, of England, and of human nature', and expressing his hope that 'American slavery (the vilest that ever saw the sun)' might soon disappear.[21] Unfortunately, the American Methodists' record of opposition to slavery in the century following Wesley's death would be checkered at best.[22]

If Wesley had one eye on developments in America, he kept the other one focused on the future of the revival in England, Scotland, Wales and Ireland. Though he would live another 15 years, he was particularly concerned from the 1770s on to make provisions for the leadership of the revival after his death. His strategy was twofold. On the one hand, he urged the preachers to sign the Articles of Agreement originally adopted in 1769, binding themselves to one another and to the Methodist standards of doctrine. On the other hand, he identified John Fletcher, a Methodist and parish priest at Madeley as his successor. Wesley implemented the first strategy, acquiring more and more signatures each year. The second strategy, however, was not to be. Despite being 26 years his senior, Wesley outlived Fletcher by more than five years.

In the meantime, the revival continued unabated. Methodism in particular grew steadily, with new societies springing up throughout the country and abroad. In 1777, Wesley himself oversaw the construction of a new chapel at City Road in London. At more than 70 years old, he continued to be an active and effective leader of the movement with which he had now been associated for 40 years.

Among the positive benefits of Wesley's age was the fact that he outlived most of his harshest critics. On the downside, as we have just seen, he also outlived some of the people who were most qualified to succeed him as the leader of the Methodist movement. Also on the downside was the fact that there were now almost four hundred Methodist preaching-houses. To his credit, Wesley recognized that, with this many preaching-houses, there were limits to how much he could do. Thus, as much as he enjoyed a good theological argument, he increasingly focused his attention on matters of oversight, delegating some of the hard and time-consuming work of theological and apologetic writing to his most trusted colleagues. For example, when he determined that Joseph Priestley's denials of the divinity of Jesus desperately needed to be addressed, Wesley asked Fletcher to do the work. When Fletcher died midway through the project, Wesley assigned the task of completing it to Joseph Benson.[23]

Though still of able body and mind, Wesley was clearly not the whirlwind of energy that he been in his younger days. Fortunately, additional help arrived in the person of Thomas Coke, who would later become known as 'the Apostle of Methodism'. An ordained Anglican priest and missionary, Coke came to London to assist Wesley in a variety of tasks, the most important of which was the writing of a legal deed of declaration. The purpose of this deed, which Coke helped Wesley to draw up in 1784, was to provide legal instructions for the organization and oversight of the conference and therefore of the societies and preaching-houses after Wesley's death.

In what would prove a controversial move, Wesley did not designate a single successor. Rather, he designated 100 people, who came to be known simply as 'the legal hundred'. These individuals, chosen by Wesley himself, would constitute the conference after John and Charles Wesley's deaths. In other words, authority was to be located in and exercised exclusively by the conference. The deed also set term limits for membership in the conference and gave clear instructions for replacing members when their terms expired.

The deed of declaration was controversial precisely because it limited the membership of the conference. Coke himself wanted the conference to be open to all of the preachers, and he let this be known. There was even a letter written on behalf of the preachers who had been excluded from the legal 100, requesting Wesley to reconsider his decision. A few of the excluded preachers went so far as to leave the movement over the issue. Despite these protests, Wesley stood firm. The deed, as they say, was done. The future leadership of the Methodist movement in England was now secure.

The entire time that Wesley was working to make provisions for the organization and leadership of Methodism after his death, he was also attempting to oversee the societies in America. Thus in 1783 Wesley designated Francis Asbury as his General Assistant, effectively putting him in charge of American Methodism. Wesley also urged the American Methodists at this time to adopt and abide by the same standards of doctrine and discipline as their counterparts in England, namely, the *Notes Upon the New Testament*, the *Sermons*, and the *Minutes* (of the Conference). The American Methodists agreed to all of these things at their annual conference in April of the following year.

As Wesley was soon to discover, however, the American and English contexts in which Methodism was now operating were markedly different. The American victory in the War for Independence entailed independence from the English crown and with it from the Church of England as well. Consequently, the Church of England was proving increasingly reluctant to send ordained priests to America. Of course, even if this had not been the case, there was also the matter that the Americans were reluctant to be baptized by and to receive the sacraments from representatives of the Church of England. Thus it was fast becoming clear to Wesley that the

Methodists in America would not be able to depend on the Church of England for the means of grace.

Ironically, it can be argued that it was precisely Wesley's Anglican sensibilities concerning the importance of the sacraments that led him to take steps that many, both in his day and ever since, have viewed as constituting separation from the Church of England. Time and again throughout his life and ministry, Wesley insisted on the spiritual vitality of the sacraments. In doing so, he proved himself an Anglican to the core. As such, the news from Asbury that many of the Methodists in America had not been baptized and that those who had been rarely, if ever, received Holy Communion struck particularly hard. In this moment, Wesley concluded against the advice of virtually everyone around him that a drastic situation required drastic measures. Thus he took it upon himself to ordain Thomas Coke a 'Superintendent' (an alternative translation for the Greek word that is otherwise translated 'bishop'), granting him power to ordain others, and together with Coke, he ordained Richard Whatcoat and Thomas Vasey as deacons and then as elders. Wesley then dispatched all of them to America, together with everything needed to start a new church apart from the Church of England, including a prayer book for worship and Articles of Religion.

As things turned out, Francis Asbury was not prepared simply to accept and implement Wesley's instructions. Thus, in a decidedly American spirit, Asbury insisted that all of the preachers in America would have to approve Wesley's plan in a conference. Moreover, Asbury suggested that, if the conference agreed to it, he and Coke would serve together as superintendents. Thus the so-called Christmas Conference was held, beginning Christmas Eve in Baltimore, Maryland in the year 1784. With a few minor exceptions and additions (Asbury was made co-superintendent with Coke), the result of the conference was the establishment of the Methodist Episcopal Church in America in accordance with the plan provided by Wesley.

In the days and weeks that followed, Wesley dealt with a significant amount of backlash from among the Methodists in England. Most notably, his brother Charles was outraged by the ordinations, writing the following satirical poem about John's actions:

So easily are Bishops made
    By man's or woman's whim?
W[esley] his hands on C[oke] hath laid,
    But who laid hands on him?

Charles also satirized Coke's ordination of Asbury, saying,

A Roman emperor, 'tis said,
    His favorite horse a consul made;

But Coke brings other things to pass.
He makes a bishop of an a--.[24]

Despite the backlash, Wesley remained convinced that he had done nothing that constituted separation from the Church of England. In fact, almost as though to emphasize that the ordinations for America did not imply separation, Wesley ordained three ministers for the revival in Scotland the following year. Once again, he pointed out that he had only ordained ministers to work in places where the Church of England was not the established church. He even went so far as to insist that no one whom he had ordained could exercise their office while in England. Nevertheless, Charles in particular continued to insist that John's actions constituted separation.

The last years of Wesley's life were marked by a combination of holding on and letting go. In many ways, Wesley held on to his role as the leader of the Methodist societies in England until the very end, writing and publishing, preaching and collecting money, and providing oversight at the annual conferences. He also held on to his contention that Methodism was nothing more and nothing less than a renewal movement within the Church of England. Thus as late as 1789 he revised the *Minutes* of the conference so as to indicate explicitly that the Methodists were 'not to form any new sect'.[25] Similarly, he held to his conviction that he was himself unfailing in his loyalty to the Church of England, saying, 'I am a Church-of-England man; and, as I said fifty years ago so I say still, in the Church I will live and die, unless I am thrust out.'[26]

Letting go proved more difficult. In 1787, Wesley was forced to let go of the American Methodists, who had, in refusing Wesley's instructions to ordain Richard Whatcoat, rather unceremoniously told Wesley to mind his own business. Indeed, the American Methodists went so far as to remove the clause from the conference *Minutes* in which they had pledged to obey Wesley's commands. When Asbury himself insisted that Wesley was not his superior, Wesley responded that the two now had 'no connexion' with one another.[27]

In 1788, John had to let go of his younger brother Charles. Though their relationship had been strained for years, the two had spent the better part of a century working side by side in the revival. Charles' death shook John to the core. Two weeks after Charles passed away, in an uncharacteristic display of emotion, Wesley broke down in tears in the middle of a service he was leading in Bolton.

Around this time, Wesley began letting go of his own health. Thus from the late 1780s on, he began making occasional references to his failing eyesight and memory. However, he almost always hastened to add a note of thanksgiving that, despite the many signs of old age, he was still able to write and preach.

When the time came to let go of his life, Wesley did so with elegance and grace. On 1 March 1791, while lying in a very weak state, he managed to sing Isaac Watts' hymn, 'I'll praise my Maker while I've breath.' When he had finished singing, he reassured those who were with him, saying, 'The best of all is, God is with us.' The next morning, he departed this life with a simple 'Farewell.'[28] Four years later, with the passing of the Plan of Pacification, the British Methodists separated from the Church of England.

CHAPTER TWO

KEEPING TO THE CHURCH:
THE STABILIZATION OF ENGLISH SOCIETY

We believe Christ to be the Eternal Supreme God; and herein we are distinguished from the Socinians and Arians. But as to all opinions which do not strike at the root of Christianity, we 'think and let think'.

John Wesley, 'The Character of a Methodist'

What, if anything, did the Methodists' separation from the Church of England say about John Wesley? Did Wesley purposely prepare the way for separation prior to his death? Did Wesley's ordaining Thomas Coke a bishop constitute a *de facto* separation from the established church? Was Wesley a faithful Anglican clergyman, or was he a rogue priest who appealed to the established church when it was convenient to do so but otherwise routinely ignored its boundaries? These are just some of the questions raised by the brief biography in Chapter One.

To date, the overwhelming tendency among scholars has been to call into question or flatly to deny the sincerity of Wesley's commitment to the Church of England. In this chapter, we will examine their reasons for doing so. Among other things, we will see that perceptions of Wesley's relationship to the established church depend to no small degree on the background assumption that eighteenth-century English church and society was already deeply secular. However, we will also notice that, on this assumption, scholars have not been able to get their story straight concerning Wesley. Thus some scholars read him as a reactionary set against secularization, while others view him as a progressive religious thinker who took secularization in stride. Having observed this disagreement, we will suggest that the problem has more to do with the assumption that eighteenth-century English church and society was deeply secular than with Wesley. Thus we will provide an alternative reading of eighteenth-century English church and society, in the light of which we will contend that Wesley was neither a reactionary nor a progressive, but a representative eighteenth-century Anglican. With this map of the terrain ahead in place, the time has come to examine popular and scholarly perceptions of Wesley's relationship to the Church of England.

POPULAR AND SCHOLARLY PERCEPTIONS

As much as any figure in the history of Christianity, popular perceptions of John Wesley revolve around a series of stories about his life, most of which have been captured in visual images across the years. For example, there is the image of a young Wesley being rescued from the Epworth rectory fire, a sure sign of divine providence at work.[1] Next, an image of Wesley anxiously weathering the storm on the high seas depicts a young man existentially suspended between faith and doubt, an experience with which many people can readily relate. Then there is the story of Wesley's heart-warming experience at Aldersgate, the very language of which has helped to focus evangelical piety on the inward dimensions of the life of faith.[2] Last but not least, there are the images of Wesley travelling on horseback and preaching to large crowds in the open air, both a source of inspiration and a challenge for people contemplating the rigours of Christian ministry.

For better or worse, the stories and images around which popular perceptions of John Wesley revolve are completely lacking in one respect. Put simply, there is no story or image that captures the significance of Wesley's relationship to the Church of England. The result of this gap in iconography is predictable. In the popular mind, John Wesley is a prototype for a form of personal piety that is disconnected from the sacramental life of the church. According to this form of piety, what matters most is not whether one is faithful to the church, but whether one is faithful to God.[3]

Somewhat surprisingly, this popular perception of Wesley is not altogether different from scholarly perceptions of Wesley. To be sure, many scholars have recognized the importance of Wesley's relationship to the established church. For example, in his now classic work, *John Wesley and the Church of England*, Frank Baker writes,

> It would be impossible to write an adequate history of the Church of England without devoting a chapter to John Wesley and the movement of which he was the centre. Nor can Wesley himself be understood apart from the Established Church. It was not simply that he happened to be born an Anglican, and from that base began to erect a new denomination, founding Methodism in reaction against his mother church. In thought and affection, in habit and atmosphere, *his whole being was inextricably interwoven with that of the church.* . . . His religious thought and practice were conceived in terms of loyalty or disloyalty to the Church of England.[4]

In a more recent essay, Jeremy Gregory insists that Wesley's relationship with the established church was the 'major theme' of his life and ministry.[5] There is even a ready willingness on the part of many scholars to recognize that Wesley resisted repeated pressures from some of the Methodist preachers to grant them permission to administer the sacraments or to separate from the Church of England. Moreover, scholars routinely call attention to the fact that, late in his life, when the pressure to separate was strongest, Wesley declared in a sermon specifically directed against schism, 'I am now, and have been from my youth, a member and a minister of the Church of England. And I have no desire nor design to separate from it till my soul separates from my body.'[6] Many scholars also cite passages from Wesley's personal correspondence in which he clearly affirms his allegiance to the Church of England and denies with equal clarity any intention to separate from it. Indeed, three such passages are particularly well-known. First, in a letter written 22 May 1750 to Gilbert Boyce, Wesley said plainly,

> But here is your grand mistake: you think my design is 'to form a Church'. No: I have no such design. It is not my design or desire that any who accept of my help should leave the Church of which they are now member.[7]

Second, in a letter written to Joseph Taylor on 16 January 1783, by which time Wesley was clearly exasperated by the issue, he asserted,

> In my Journals, in the *Magazine*, in every possible way, I have advised the Methodists to keep to the Church. They that do this most prosper best in their souls; I have observed it long. If ever the Methodists in general were to leave the Church, I must leave them.[8]

Third, and most famously, in a letter written on 6 May 1788 to Henry Moore, an aged Wesley declared for all posterity, 'I am a Church-of-England man; . . . In the Church I will live and die, unless I am thrust out.'[9]

How, then, do scholars support popular perceptions of Wesley as someone not deeply dependent upon the established church? On the face of things, it appears that scholarly perceptions differ markedly from popular perceptions. Suffice it to say, recognizing that Wesley's life was inextricably intertwined with the life of the established Church does not amount to arguing that Wesley viewed the established church favourably, much less that he saw his own life and work as deeply dependent upon it. Similarly, citing Wesley's own words in support of the Church of England does not amount to taking Wesley at his word.

As things turn out, many scholars interpret Wesley's repeated claims that he was 'a Church of England man' as either self-deception or outright disingenuousness. They insist that a discrepancy exists between what Wesley *said* concerning his relationship to the Church of England and what he actually *did* throughout his life and ministry. For example, Joseph Beaumont once quipped, 'Mr. Wesley, like a strong and skilful rower, looked one way, while every stroke of his oar took him in the opposite direction.'[10] Even Frank Baker, whose work related Wesley to the established church more positively than any before or since, observed, 'Whatever deliberate separation from the Church of England took place during Wesley's ministry was primarily in the realm of deeds rather than of thought.'[11] More recently, David Hempton has argued that Wesley's support of the Church of England was 'always more impressive in thought than in deed'.[12] Thus Jeremy Gregory is exactly right when he says, 'A common reading of what he did presents us with a Wesley, who despite his own protestations, showed how little he cared for the church.'[13]

Behind this common reading lies a network of background assumptions about the status and health of the Church of England in the eighteenth century. The upshot of these assumptions is that the established church was in bad shape. For example, Maldwyn Edwards claims that Wesley was 'a rebel in thought as well as in action', and that 'only a sleepy, loosely disciplined Church would have tolerated his shock tactics so long'.[14] Frank Baker agrees, saying,

> The Church of England in Wesley's day was not only lax in the ordering of worship and in pastoral oversight. At the higher levels of church government, there was little co-ordination of responsibilities; ecclesiastical authority had become an empty show, and spiritual initiative dissipated itself in political maneuvering. . . . As the enfeebled church faltered, so did the power of the state grow, and during Wesley's long lifetime a maturing parliamentary government laid hands on many powers not only of the crown but of the church.[15]

Taken together, scholarly judgements that Wesley's actions undermined his words and that the Church of England in the eighteenth century was lax, corrupt and spiritually compromised serve to reinforce the popular image of Wesley described above. Surely we are dealing here with someone who, recognizing that the church was corrupt to the core, did whatever it took to help people come to know and to love God, a virtual one-man evangelistic enterprise. Surely Wesley's life and ministry reflect how bad things really were in the established church. Surely by the end of his life, if not well before, he was dreaming of starting his own church.

In order to set the stage for a revisionist account of Wesley's relationship to the Church of England, we need to take a closer look at the relationship between the widespread perception that Wesley was either indifferent or even hostile toward the church and the background assumption that, in the eighteenth century, the Church of England was in serious decline.

Once we have done this, we will turn our attention to the recent scholarly reassessment of eighteenth-century English church and society, on the basis of which we will provide a revised account of Wesley's relationship to the established church – an account that will support Wesley's claim to be 'a Church of England man'. We will suggest that, far from reflecting the corruption and decline of the Church of England in the eighteenth century, Wesley's life and ministry can be seen as a testimony to its wisdom, flexibility and vitality, and that Wesley himself should be seen neither as a 'rebel' nor as the founder of his own church, but as a representative eighteenth-century Anglican.

THE SECULARIZATION THESIS

Until recently, it has been assumed that eighteenth-century English church and society were witnesses to a massive cultural transition from a confessional to an increasingly secular state. At the heart of this transition were things like the undermining of revealed religion, the decay of the established Church, the rise of popular sovereignty and rampant irreligion and immorality. Let us refer to this once dominant line of interpretation simply as the *secularization thesis*.

According to the secularization thesis, eighteenth-century England, while not nearly as unstable and violent as the preceding century, was plagued by a deep and widespread cultural transition from a confessional state to what scholars refer to by turns as the age of reason, the modern age, the early industrial age, the English enlightenment, and the like.[16] To be sure, the eighteenth-century English enlightenment was significantly less bloody than its French counterpart. Nonetheless, the forces of secularization combined to call into question and ultimately to undermine confidence in revealed religion – the very foundation upon which English church and society had for so long depended for authority and for order.

What were these secularizing forces that were undermining the very foundations of English church and society? There is something of a standard list that can be seen in a wide variety of interpreters. Especially interesting is the fact that most of the items on this list show up in interpreters who, while agreeing in their assessment of eighteenth-century English society, draw opposite conclusions about both the role and the impact of Wesley and the Evangelical revival in that setting. Thus, as we will see, Wesley can be viewed in light of the secularization thesis either as a hero or as a goat, as a proto-modernist or as a reactionary determined to turn back the clock to pre-modern times. For now, we need to acquaint ourselves with five secularizing forces purportedly at work in eighteenth-century English church and society.

The first and most often mentioned secularizing force is natural or rational religion. The boogeyman here is Deism. Deists persistently sought to undermine revealed religion by making reason the rule of faith and by disallowing appeals to mystery and divine intervention. Especially influential Deist works included John Toland's *Christianity Not Mysterious* (1695) and Matthew Tindal's *Christianity as Old as Creation* (1730). However, it is not simply the publication of these works that makes the eighteenth century appear increasingly secular, but the fact that neither the church nor the state appears to have been especially determined to stop the spread of Deism. For example, the fact that Tindal 'was comfortably ensconced as a Fellow of All Souls College' at Oxford can be seen as evidence that church and state alike were increasingly secular.[17]

A second secularizing force is another form of rational religion, namely, Socinianism or Unitarianism.[18] Like the Deists, Socinians and Unitarians rejected the Trinity and the divinity of Jesus Christ. And while Unitarians allowed for mysteries 'not contrary to reason', the category turned out to be an empty one. Among eighteenth-century Unitarians, none was more controversial than Joseph Priestley, who published numerous popular works denying the divinity of Christ, the virgin birth and other sacred doctrines of revealed religion.

A third secularizing force has to do with the perception of a growing gap between the church and the state. As evidence of such a gap, interpreters of eighteenth-century English society frequently point to the Toleration Act of 1689, as a result of which the church lost its power to compel church attendance. In addition, there was the matter of Whig anti-clericalism in the 1730s, as a result of which the church gradually lost its power to function as moral police in English society.[19]

A fourth secularizing force is frequently said to occur in the area of political philosophy. Scholars often suggest that the influence of social contract theory and appeals for popular sovereignty were on the rise throughout the eighteenth century, gradually undermining commitment to the constitutional monarchy from within. Moreover, it is customary to see a close connection between Deism and Socinianism on the one hand, and the Whig opposition to the church and the increasing commitment to popular sovereignty on the other. In other words, anti-Trinitarianism, opposition to ecclesiastical authority, and democratic sentiment formed a close-knit nexus of secularizing forces.[20]

A fifth secularizing force has to do with the ongoing work of natural philosophy, the success of which meant that people were no longer dependent (if they ever had been) on revealed religion to understand and to navigate the natural world.[21] In some circles, most notably the Royal Society, success in natural philosophy fuelled a robust optimism about the potential of scientific inquiry to solve an entire range of problems and a profound sense that the problems themselves existed because of a dependence on revealed religion for information about the natural world. Most telling, however, is the fact that a large number of clergy were active and enthusiastic participants in applied natural philosophy. It is simply assumed that, if clergy were engaging in the work of natural philosophy, then they must have had increasing reservations about revealed religion.[22]

At this stage, many adherents of the secularization thesis turn their attention to the effects of secularizing forces. Once again, there is a standard list, at the top of which is the perception of rampant immorality at all levels of society. Most troubling has been the perception of immorality among the clergy and among members of the Episcopal bench, whom J. Wesley Bready once described as 'spiritually unbaptized'.[23] Indeed, Bready perceives the closest relationship between the secularizing forces outlined above and the moral and spiritual degeneracy of the church. Thus he writes,

> Beneath the polished surface of deistic rationalism, the springs of spiritual life were running dry: and the Church, having no impelling Faith or guiding philosophy of her own, degenerated not only into a confessed branch of the Civil Service, but into a public sounding-board, which re-echoed the glib phraseology of the new and heady 'sciences' of Political Arithmetic and Natural Philosophy.[24]

In addition to perceptions of immorality and spiritual degeneracy within the Church and among the clergy, the standard list of the effects of secularizing forces includes an entire host of moral and social problems in English society. Among the most commonly noted are the barbarity of the prison system, addictions to gin and gambling, rampant sexual immorality, the profaneness of the theatre, the poverty of the lower classes, the abuse of children, and England's role in the slave trade. Such were the birth pangs of the modern age. Whatever secularization would eventually achieve, the transition from a confessional state to an age of science, free market capitalism and democracy brought with it a new catalogue of personal and social vices.

At this stage, two evaluative comments concerning the secularization thesis are in order. First, many aspects of the secularization thesis are supported by a wide range of primary sources. For example, with regard to the undermining of revealed religion, Thomas Secker, the future archbishop of Canterbury, complained,

> . Christianity is now railed at and ridiculed with very little reserve, and its teachers without any at all. Against us our adversaries appear to have set themselves to be as bitter as they can, not only beyond all truth, but beyond all probability, exaggerating without mercy.[25]

With regard to the notion that eighteenth-century English church and society was morally and spiritually degenerate, Joseph Trapp, an Oxford High Churchman, lamented, 'I presume it will be allowed by everybody that all manner of wickedness, both in principles and in practice, abounds among us to a degree unheard of since Christianity was in being.'[26] Similarly, Bishop George Berkeley, not normally prone to overstatement, described the moral state of affairs in early eighteenth-century England in almost apocalyptic terms, referring not to an age of reason but to an 'age of monsters'. Thus he bemoaned,

> Our prospect is very terrible and the symptoms grow worse from day to day. . . . The youth born and brought up in wicked times without any bias to good from early principle, or instilled opinion, when they grow ripe, must be monsters indeed. And it is to be feared that the age of monsters is not far off.[27]

Second, it must be said that the secularization thesis often fails to note the extent to which secularizing forces were at work primarily among social and intellectual elites. Thus radicalism and freethinking tended to flourish in salons, coffeehouses and pubs among the so-called 'leisure classes'.[28] There is little evidence that these forces were rampant among the urban working class or in rural areas. At the same time, one could argue that the working class was not altogether untouched by modernizing forces if indeed one of those forces was a loss of power on the part of the established church to require church attendance and to enforce morality. Thus John Walsh observes, 'The collier colonies – like those at Kingswood, soon to be visited by Whitefield and Wesley – were regarded as spectacularly ignorant of things spiritual.' Walsh continues,

> Lord Egmont was astonished by the godlessness of the miners near Bristol in 1733. He was told that a local gentleman interrogating them about their absence from church had exclaimed, 'Why . . . I believe you know nothing of the Commandments.' To this, 'they replied they knew such a family living in their parts, but they did not know them personally.'[29]

A great deal more can be said about the relative strengths and weaknesses of the secularization thesis. For example, there is a deep inconsistency in the secularization thesis as it relates to the established church. On the one hand, the Whig Ascendency is supposed to have rendered the established church powerless. On the other hand, adherents of the secularization thesis often criticize the church for failing to do anything about irreligion and immorality in eighteenth-century English society. Suffice it to say, advocates of the secularization thesis cannot have it both ways. Either the Church of England was powerless and therefore cannot be held accountable for immorality and irreligion in society, or the established church retained a considerable amount of power and influence throughout the century yet did little to stave off the rising tide of irreligion and immorality. Leaving this aside for the moment, we need to see how the secularization thesis has informed interpretations of the relationship between Wesley and the Church of England.

Wesley as Reactionary and Proto-Modernist

In many ways, Wesley makes for great sound bites in support of the secularization thesis. For example, he lamented that Deism had 'overspread all Europe', and he described the deists themselves as 'mere beasts in human shape, wholly under the power of the basest passions'.[30] Similarly, Wesley warned about the increase of irreligion generally and about indifference among Christians in particular, observing that there were 'enthusiasts in the cause of impiety' who took 'more pains to make converts to irreligion than many Christians, however sincere in their profession', were willing to take 'to defend the holy faith delivered to them'.[31] Moreover, Wesley discerned no small amount of immorality and corruption in the established church, inveighing against the 'indolent clergymen, pleasure-taking clergymen, money-loving clergymen, praise-loving clergymen, preferment-seeking clergymen' who were, not to put too fine a point on it, 'a stink in the nostrils of God'.[32]

This is, of course, a mere sampling. We could easily produce hundreds of quotes from Wesley of a similar kind. The point here is to see that Wesley can appear to be a ready witness for the secularization thesis. Not surprisingly, this is precisely how many scholars have interpreted him across the years. In one way or another, they have read Wesley primarily in relation to the forces of secularization in English church and society.

What *is* surprising is that, while most scholars read Wesley in light of the secularization thesis, they often draw opposite conclusions about how Wesley fits within that thesis. In other words, scholars who agree that eighteenth-century England was increasingly secular tend to disagree rather sharply about how to locate Wesley vis-à-vis the forces of secularization. On the one hand, many scholars read Wesley as a reactionary figure who rejected the forces of secularization in their entirety. On the other hand, a growing number of scholars read him as a proto-modernist figure who led the way in helping Christianity adapt to the forces of secularization, most notably democratic sentiment and the growing separation of church and state in political philosophy, and the empirical method in natural philosophy. Given the sharp contrast between these two ways of locating Wesley within the wider horizon of the secularization thesis, we should take a moment to explore them in greater detail.

The first and more traditional option is to view Wesley as a reactionary figure set over against the secularizing forces in English church and society. On this view, Wesley is swimming upstream the whole way. Indeed, things were so bad all around that he had to start his own movement, if not his own church. The established church was simply too far gone, a victim of secularization. Consequently, Wesley and his colleagues in the revival were willing to use any means necessary to get the job done, including field and lay preaching, holding alternative services, and the like. If this meant ignoring parish boundaries, then so be it. Desperate times called for desperate measures. Wesley was simply not willing to wait for the established church to get its act together.

Depending on one's perspective, this way of locating Wesley and the evangelical revival amid the swirling forces of secularization can make him either a hero or a goat. From the perspective of scholars who view secularization in terms of intellectual, political and cultural progress, Wesley is a reactionary, anti-Enlightenment figure trying desperately to turn back the clock to a more naïve and oppressive age. For example, Leslie Stephen complained that Wesley believed in 'popular superstitions' such as the Devil, which, 'in the eighteenth century had become, even amongst the vulgar, a rather more shadowy being than he had been in an earlier generation'. Moreover, noted Stephen, Wesley believed in miracles so strongly that he was constantly making reference to 'some direct miraculous interference'. Worst of all, he clearly had an 'aversion to scientific reasoning,' disbelieving in Newtonian astronomy and calling into question 'the whole framework of modern astronomy'.[33] More recently, E. P. Thompson decried the evangelical revival as essentially 'a movement of counter-enlightenment,' citing the fact that Wesley affirmed 'bibliomancy, old wives' medical remedies, the casting of lots, the belief in diabolical possession and in exorcism by prayer, in the hand of providence', and belief in 'the punishment (by lightning-stroke, or epilepsy, or cholera) of ill-livers and reprobates'.[34]

By contrast, from the perspective of advocates for revealed religion, Wesley is a hero of messianic proportions, defending Christianity from the secularizing forces in English church and society. Together with those who worked alongside him in the revival, Wesley was a vital witness for God in a rationalistic and increasingly atheistic age. Once again, Bready is typical:

> Wesley's supreme purpose was to make men vitally conscious of God. . . . With prophetic insight he recognised the insidious demons which were luring millions of his countrymen into the tangled labyrinths of moral corruption and spiritual death: and challenging the sway of those demons, he set about to release the victims from their woeful plight. He saw the ecclesiastical machinery of his generation rusty and clogged with dust. . . . His purpose was not to formulate a new theology or a new theory of Church or State, but to touch dead bones with the breath of spiritual power, and make them live; to release the winds of heaven, that they might blow upon the ashy embers of religion and kindle a purging, illuminating fire of righteousness and truth.[35]

41

The second major option for viewing Wesley within the horizon of the secularization thesis contrasts starkly with the first. Whereas the first group of scholars views Wesley as a reactionary, anti-Enlightenment figure, a second, more recent, group of scholars reads him as a highly creative proto-modern thinker who purposely adapted Christianity to many of the secularizing forces described above.[36] For example, over against older notions of divine institution and compulsory membership, Frederick Dreyer argues that 'the belief that societies were artificial and existed only by virtue of their members' consent formed one of the orthodoxies of the eighteenth century.'[37] Moreover, this belief clearly extended beyond the religious societies to the church itself. After all, as early as 1689, John Locke had declared,

> A church, then, I take to be a voluntary society of men, joining them-selves together of their own accord in order to the public worshipping of God in such manner as they judge acceptable to him, and effectual to the salvation of their souls.[38]

According to Dreyer, Wesley agreed with Locke wholeheartedly, regarding the church as 'a voluntary association that derived all the legitimacy it possessed from the agreement of its members'. Moreover, says Dreyer, Wesley clearly 'rejected the church ideal of a compulsory membership'. Thus he concludes, 'However dictatorial Wesley may have been in his direction of Methodism, he always recognized that consent was the foundation of his authority.' In this respect, Wesley was anything but a reactionary. On the contrary, he was among those most ready and willing to apply the central tenets of early modern political philosophy 'without confusion or inconsistency' to the church.[39]

Even more comprehensively than Dreyer, David Bebbington has argued that Wesley and the evangelical revival are best understood as 'an adaptation of the Protestant tradition through contact with the Enlightenment'.[40] Recognizing that the revival 'has often been read as a reaction against a tide of rationalism', Bebbington insists this was not 'Wesley's own estimate of the matter', and quotes Wesley from one of his letters: 'It is a fundamental principle with us that to renounce reason is to renounce religion, that religion and reason go hand in hand, and that all irrational religion is false religion.'[41]

For Bebbington, the wider 'Evangelical movement' of which Wesley was a part was 'permeated by Enlightenment influences'.[42] Indeed, the whole cast of Wesley's mind was 'moulded by the new intellectual currents of his time'. As evidence for this claim, Bebbington points to the fact that Wesley was 'supremely . . . an empiricist' and that he was committed to a range of specific Enlightenment ideas, including religious tolerance, free will and anti-slavery.[43] Furthermore, in keeping with natural philosophy,

Wesley had an 'anti-metaphysical bent', being committed to 'the testing of hypotheses by observation'.[44] Rounding off his account, Bebbington says that Wesley and the evangelicals reflected the Enlightenment 'in their optimistic temper' and in their commitment to the principle that 'God wished human beings to be happy'.[45] After all, Wesley routinely talked not simply of holiness, but of *happiness* and *holiness.*

It is interesting to note that the opposing views of Wesley that emerge in light of the secularization thesis imply rather different views of the Church of England as well. More specifically, they explain why the revival was needed in the first place by drawing, however subtly, opposing inferences about what was wrong with the Church of England. On the one hand, scholars who interpret Wesley and the revival as reactionary often suggest that the problem with the Church of England was that it had been eroded both from without and from within by the secularizing forces of the age. Put simply, the Church of England was increasingly secular. On the other hand, scholars who interpret Wesley as a proto-modernist often imply that the problem with the Church of England was that it was stuck in old patterns of thinking, favouring as it did hierarchy, divine right institutionalism, the authority of divine revelation and the like. Put simply, the Church of England was beset by its own inertia.

Suffice it to say, there is a serious problem of interpretation here. Wesley cannot be both a reactionary seeking to turn back the clock and a progressive determined to adapt Christianity to the modern age. Moreover, the Church of England can not be both thoroughly secular and holding on for dear life to divine right institutionalism. At this stage, the easy thing to do would be to choose one of these ways of reading Wesley. A more interesting way to go, however, is to call the secularization thesis itself into question. After all, this is what these otherwise opposing views have in common. By doing so, we will make possible an entirely different way of thinking about Wesley's relationship to the Church of England.

THE ANGLICAN STABILIZATION THESIS

In recent years, three scholarly developments have combined to call into question the secularization thesis, especially as it applies to the Church of England in the eighteenth century. First, a growing number of scholars have observed that the historiography of eighteenth-century English church and society has been unduly influenced by the sweeping negative assessments of the established church's eighteenth-century critics, including Wesley, and by the equally sweeping and at times even harsher judgements of the established church's nineteenth-century critics, most notably the tractarians of the Oxford Movement.[46] In other words, until recently, eighteenth-century English church and society has been defined almost entirely by its critics. Consequently, much of the criticism levied against the established church and its leaders has consisted of generalizations and caricatures.[47]

Second, into the gap created by the growing awareness that eighteenth-century English church and society has been defined almost entirely by its critics, there has emerged an influential revisionist thesis according to which England remained a healthy confessional state throughout the 'long eighteenth century', which is to say, from the Restoration of 1660 to the Reform Act of 1832. Most closely associated with J. C. D. Clark's *English Society, 1660–1832*, this revisionist thesis rejects the notion that the Church of England was either complacent or secular. Rather, it maintains that the established church and its doctrines – most notably the doctrines of the Trinity and the atonement – were nothing less than 'the unifying principles of the social and political order'.[48]

Third, some scholars have recently criticized the confessional state thesis in a way that fills it out in an enticing direction. Generally speaking, the criticism of the confessional state thesis is that, like the secularization thesis, it resorts to sweeping generalizations, painting a picture of English church and society with a very broad brush. More specifically, the thesis is too static, making it seem as though a confessional state simply sprang into existence. Jeremy Gregory's criticism of Clark to this effect is worth quoting at length:

> In J. C. D. Clark's interpretation of events the Anglican hegemony he perceives in the intellectual sphere was matched by an almost effort-less Anglican dominance in the parishes of England. But in some ways, Clark's work seriously underestimates the problems faced by clergy in their pastoral task. It might also be suggested that Clark's analysis has done little more than to reinterpret the traditional notion of eighteenth-century stasis. Instead of seeing the period as one which saw the tri-umph of rationalism and stability over religious fanaticism, we are now asked to see a new kind of stability based on this being an age of largely unperturbed and unproblematic faith. Anglicanism, so he assumes, was unquestioned and its essential tenets seem almost magically to have percolated right down the social scale. In brief, the new eighteenth century is becoming as much of a myth as the old, a 'cosy' world where everyone shared in the same beliefs and assumptions.[49]

One way to read Gregory's criticism of Clark is to note that it is by no means an outright rejection of the confessional state thesis. Gregory is simply calling attention to the fact that the confessional state was never a *fait accompli*. On the contrary, the construction and maintenance of the confessional state met with resistance and required a great deal of polit-ical savvy and some very hard work on the ground, most notably by high-ranking clergy. Thus Gregory's own contribution to our understanding of eighteenth-century English church and society is a careful study of the work done by the clergy in the eighteenth century, including their response to and management of nonconformity and, more positively, their allowance and even encouragement of 'new religious impulses'.[50]

If we combine Clark's revisionist thesis with Gregory's analysis of the work being done on the ground, the picture that begins to emerge is one in which the Church of England played a leading role in the stabilization of English society as a confessional state throughout the long eighteenth century. On this picture, the clergy were neither idle nor secular. They were busy developing and deploying a political strategy for the reconstruction and maintenance of England as a confessional state. Let us call this the *Anglican stabilization thesis*.

Contrary to the secularization thesis, on which eighteenth-century English church and society were overrun by Deism, Socinianism and other forms of freethinking radicalism, advocates of the Anglican stabilization thesis maintain that there was a very strong commitment to the doctrine of the Trinity and to the reception of the sacraments as non-negotiable for public office, for military service, for ordination and for admission to Oxford and graduation from Cambridge.[51] Most importantly, this commitment existed at the level of church and state. After all, if the claim were simply that a few Anglican clergymen continued to urge belief in the Trinity and reception of the sacraments, it would hardly undermine the secularization thesis, a crucial part of which is the notion that the established church was disempowered by the anti-clericalism of the Whig Ascendency.

Much more is being claimed here. According to Clark and others, we have here a political theology that was shared by church and state alike. If this is true, then it constitutes a real blow for the secularization thesis, which has always depended more on the presumed secularity and anti-clericalism of the Whigs in Parliament than on the secularity and heterodoxy of the clergy. As Gerald Cragg noted many years ago, the Whigs have routinely been presented as 'defenders of dissenters and the champions of a free press', which is to say, of two of the hallmarks of secularization.

As things turn out, the Whigs viewed the church as 'a part of the constitutional settlement', and as 'a body of immense political importance whose support' needed to be won 'for the Hanoverian regime'. Cragg continues,

> Few developments in the first half of the eighteenth century were so important as the conversion of the Whig party to the support of the Establishment. The church became a prize for which politicians contended, not an issue on which they were divided.[52]

If the secularity and anti-clericalism of the Whigs is at the heart of the secularization thesis, then in many ways the Whig alliance with the established church is central to the Anglican stabilization thesis. The evidence for this alliance is particularly strong. Throughout the long eighteenth century, Parliament repeatedly refused to overturn the Act of Uniformity, as well as the Test and Corporation Acts. These acts excluded nonconformists, freethinkers and Catholics from clerical, civil and military offices by requiring subscription to the Articles of Religion and reception of the sacraments in the established church. Indeed, the Test and Corporation Acts lasted until 1828, and the Act of Uniformity was not revised until 1872.[53] Consequently, Clark rightly concludes that, backed by Parliament, an 'apostolical and sacerdotal rather than Erastian or rationalist' church was able to maintain 'its constitutional place in society'.[54]

The success of this alliance was such that nonconformists and dissenters (the very groups the Whigs were supposed to have championed) were 'consigned to a backwater of the national life', their efforts to improve their status achieving 'few results'. Indeed, as the century wore on, 'their vitality waned', and while the Act of Toleration 'acknowledged their right to exist and to worship as they wished', they clearly had a 'second-class status'.[55] John Walsh and Stephen Taylor summarize the consequences of the Whig-church alliance for nonconformity, saying, 'It was clear that Nonconformity was largely marginalized: though often perceived as a nuisance it was not seen as a threat to Anglican hegemony.'[56]

By definition, requiring belief in the Trinity and reception of the sacraments in the established church for full participation in English society ruled out precisely those groups which either rejected the Trinity or refused to receive communion in the Church of England. In other words, it was a strategy clearly intended to stabilize English church and society by marginalizing Deists, Socinians, Arians and Catholics. This, of course, raises a question. Why were those in authority in late seventeenth- and eighteenth-century England intent on marginalizing entire groups of people? These were, after all, religiously affiliated groups of people. Did anyone really think that religious groups were capable of destabilizing English society? Did anyone seriously believe that Deists, Socinians, Arians or Catholics could bring down the English government? In a word, yes.

Throughout the seventeenth century, English church and society was under constant threat of destabilization, if not destruction. As perceived by high-ranking officials in church and state alike, there were both external and internal threats to be monitored closely. In this case, perception was reality. These high-ranking officials were neither paranoid nor delusional. The threats were very real.

On the one hand, we cannot venture too far into a discussion of these threats. After all, this is a book on John Wesley. On the other hand, if we are to understand John Wesley, then we must understand the world in which he lived. Therefore we must say a word or two about what many people, including John Wesley, regarded as threats to life as they knew it.

Until the recent rise in public consciousness of militant Islamic states, most people living in the late modern West assumed that religion was a personal matter and therefore politically harmless. To be sure, religious groups sometimes lobby the governments of modern nation-states or attempt to influence the outcome of elections. Yet we have not been accustomed to worrying that the Presbyterians might take over the government and throw all of the Methodists and Anglicans out of public office or even out of their homes. Nor do we spend time worrying that if a Catholic is made President or Prime Minister the whole country over which that person presides as 'executive-in-chief' will suddenly be forced to become Catholic. In short, we are used to thinking in terms of 'the separation of church and state'.

John Wesley lived in a completely different world. In late seventeenth- and early eighteenth-century England, religious groups were never merely religious. They were always overtly political as well. Indeed, there was no need to create a special sub-discipline known as political theology.[57] All theology was political, and all politics was theological. If anything has led to a distorted view of John Wesley, it has been the tendency among Wesley studies scholars to forget this fact.[58]

What, then, were the political threats to the stability of English church and society that Parliament and high-ranking church officials were seeking to stave off by requiring confession of the Trinity and reception of the sacrament for participation in public life? Externally, the threat was never simply Catholicism as a system of belief. After all, the Church of England was purportedly half Catholic in its theology and worship. Rather, in late seventeenth- and eighteenth-century England, the mention of Catholicism almost always brought to mind the absolute monarchy and war machine of Louis XIV in France. Indeed, it would not be too much to say that throughout much of the long eighteenth century, English subjects from the highest to the lowest orders suffered from what some have called Francophobia, that is, an intense fear of the French. The greatest evidence for such a fear is, of course, the Glorious Revolution in 1688. It was not coincidental that the English deposed a Catholic king just as Louis XIV was coming into the height of his power. Nor was it an accident that, when the time came to find a successor, they turned to the most reliably Protestant people in all of Europe – namely, the Dutch. With a Protestant king in place, the requirement of the reception of the sacrament for full participation in public life prevented the likelihood of a Catholic takeover, as they say, from the bottom up.

Internally, anti-Trinitarian groups like the Deists, Arians and Socinians were perceived as threats precisely because the 'key political doctrine of subordination' on which English church and society was based was 'deduced' from 'theological first principles', most notably a hierarchical conception of the doctrine of the Trinity.[59] Conversely, anti-Trinitarianism was widely perceived as 'conceptually basic' to democratic principles. After all, anti-Trinitarian groups denied that Christ 'exercised divine authority'. By extension, they denied that Christ had instituted a priesthood which, in turn, meant a denial of the divine institution of the Church of England. Needless to say, if the church was not divinely instituted, then neither was the state. As Clark puts it, ' "No bishop, no king" was once more a relevant challenge, if mankind was free to amend or reject its ecclesiastical and political hierarchy in the name of reason, conscience or utility.'[60] Subscription to the Articles of Religion and therefore to the Trinity was thus intended not simply to preserve theological orthodoxy for orthodoxy's sake. It was also a strategy for safeguarding the principles of subordination and order upon which the whole of English society was based.

While such a strategy might seem intolerant by twenty-first-century standards, there was another side to it. The strategy for stabilization was truly twofold. On the one hand, it required all public servants to confess the Trinity and receive the sacraments, thereby excluding the Deists, Socinians, Arians and Catholics. On the other hand, it allowed considerable breathing room for a number of other groups provided that they did not deny the Trinity or refuse the sacraments. For example, there was ample breathing room for practitioners of natural philosophy. Indeed, there is little sense that natural philosophy was perceived as being incompatible with either the Trinity or the sacraments. Thus, contrary to the secularization thesis, which maintains that natural philosophy was among the forces undermining revealed religion, Clark notes that the established church exhibited 'a remarkable alliance with emergent natural science, and kept that alliance in good repair until the mid nineteenth century'.[61]

What did all of this mean for Wesley and the people called Methodists? Three brief comments are in order. First and foremost, Wesley clearly believed in the Trinity, and he personally received the sacraments with an unusually high rate of frequency.[62] Moreover, Wesley insisted that the Methodists were deeply committed to the Trinity, and he urged them to receive the sacraments in the Church of England as often as they could. Thus Wesley was committed to the very things around which the confessional state was being constructed and maintained. In this sense, he was a very strong supporter of the Anglican hegemony.

Second, there is evidence that representatives of the established church not only allowed, but sometimes even encouraged, the spread of Methodism. For example, in the late 1750s, a group of Methodists under the leadership of Edward Perronet leased their meetinghouse from the Archbishop of Canterbury. In 1761, Archbishop Secker

cautioned the curate of Minister in Shepper to 'acknowledge whatever is good in any of the Methodists; acknowledge their intention to be

KEEPING TO THE CHURCH

good . . . even when they do wrong; say nothing to the disadvantage of any of them . . .; beware of ridiculing any expression of theirs'.[63]

This is a good example of the other half of the strategy for stabilization at work. It is as though Archbishop Secker is saying, 'There are far more dangerous people to watch out for than John Wesley and the Methodists.'

Third, there is the fact that, despite all of his purportedly rebellious activities, Wesley never had his ordination revoked. On the secularization thesis, as we have seen, this fact simply reflects the laxity of the eighteenth-century established church. Due to secularization from within or disempowerment from without, the Church of England was simply too lazy to bother with disciplining or expelling someone like Wesley. On the Anglican stabilization thesis, however, the Church of England was neither secular nor disempowered. On the contrary, the established church was busy constructing and maintaining an Anglican confessional state in part by excluding extreme groups from full participation in public life, including the life of the church. Thus we are faced with an interesting choice. We can either reject the Anglican stabilization thesis in favour of the secularization thesis, or we are going to have to account for the fact that Wesley was never excommunicated from the church.

Wesley as Representative Eighteenth-Century Anglican

In suggesting that Wesley was a representative eighteenth-century Anglican, we will be swimming upstream. As we have seen, there is something approaching a scholarly consensus that Wesley did too many things unbecoming an Anglican priest to be representative of Anglicanism. Whatever he might have said concerning his devotion to the established church, his actions clearly betrayed him. Or did they?

In the remainder of this chapter, we will do two things. First, we will identify and re-evaluate the major forms of evidence often cited by scholars who read Wesley either as a bad excuse for an Anglican or as an outright separatist. On this front, we will identify and re-evaluate the activities that supposedly undermine Wesley's claims to be deeply committed to the established church – namely, field preaching, establishing societies, the use of lay leaders and preachers, and the ordaining of Thomas Coke and others for America and Scotland. We will then consider the fact that other ordained Anglican clergy often objected to Wesley's actions and queried whether or not he was truly committed to the church, suggesting an alternative way of thinking about the role of public criticism in eighteenth-century England, as well as an alternative way of understanding the differences between John and Charles Wesley concerning the importance of the Church of England relative to Methodism. Next, we will readily acknowledge that Wesley was an especially harsh critic of the Church of

England, but we will suggest that there is more than one way to understand this aspect of Wesley's life and work. Finally, we will observe that scholars have begun to re-assess whether Wesley's belief in miracles, demonic possession and the like is evidence that he was increasingly out of step with eighteenth-century English church and society.

Second, having identified and re-evaluated the evidence most often cited against Wesley's claims to be deeply committed to the established church, we will make a case that Wesley was, by eighteenth-century standards, a representative Anglican. Initially, we will suggest that the character of eighteenth-century Anglicanism can be seen in the failure of the episcopacy to take action against Wesley. With the Anglican stabilization thesis and against the secularization thesis, we will maintain that this failure to take action is a witness not to laxity and corruption, but to the wisdom, flexibility and vitality of the eighteenth-century established church. More importantly, we will observe that the failure to discipline Wesley was in keeping with eighteenth-century Anglican political theology. Finally, we will contend that, in the light of this political theology, Wesley was a representative Anglican, and that the best evidence for this is to be found, ironically, in his administration of the Methodist movement. For now, the time has come to re-evaluate the evidence most often cited to support the notion that Wesley was not deeply committed to the Church of England.

As we saw near the outset of this chapter, scholars often portray Wesley as a rebellious cleric. They routinely claim that, despite his repeated affirmations of loyalty to the Church of England, Wesley's actions finally speak louder than his words. But what were these actions that made Wesley such a rebel? What, precisely, did he do that so thoroughly compromised his testimony concerning his devotion to the established church?

Generally speaking, scholars most frequently point to Wesley's involvement in field preaching, the establishment of religious societies, the use of lay leaders and preachers, and the ordination of ministers for ministry in America and Scotland.[64] We can dispatch with the first three of these activities rather easily by noting that they did not break canon laws and that, quite apart from the evangelical revival, there was precedent in the Church of England in each case. For example, there were prominent Anglican clergymen who were not associated with the revival and yet who were known to preach outdoors. George Horne, who was dean of Canterbury and later bishop of Norwich, was known to preach outside while he was president of Magdallen College, Oxford, 'the better, he said, to emulate John the Baptist'.[65] Similarly, it is well established that the Church of England sponsored religious societies within its parishes long before the evangelical revival began, most notably the Society for Promoting Christian Knowledge (founded 1698) and the Society for the Propagation of the Gospel (founded 1701), as well as various societies for the reformation of manners.[66] Likewise, the use of lay leaders in the work of ministry was not without precedent outside the revival. This includes, albeit in an indirect way, the involvement of lay leaders in the work of preaching. Samuel Johnson was known to have written sermons for ordained clergy to preach; indeed, Norman Sykes once observed that one of the hallmarks of the Georgian church was the 'laicization of religion'.[67] Suffice it to say, then, that while Wesley was more involved in these things than most, field preaching, the use of lay leaders and religious societies were hardly anti-establishment activities.

Before we take up the more controversial matter of Wesley's ordinations, an additional comment is in order. Among other things, the fact that the Church of England sponsored religious societies helps to show that it was not nearly as lax and unmotivated as the secularization thesis often suggests. This lends additional support to the Anglican stabilization thesis. It also means that Elie Halevy's famous thesis that Wesley and the evangelical revival saved England from a violent revolution must be carefully qualified.[68] Indeed, if the Anglican stabilization thesis is correct, and if Wesley was on those terms a representative Anglican, then the Halevy thesis clearly needs to be revised. If anything saved England from a violent revolution (it is possible to argue that the conditions for a violent revolution were never there in the first place), then it may well have been the Church of England's role in the construction and maintenance of a confessional state – which in turn allowed Wesley and the evangelical revival not simply to exist but to flourish.

What, then, are we to make of Wesley's ordaining persons as elders and, in at least one case, as a bishop, for ministry in America and Scotland? If ever Wesley violated canon law, then surely it was in claiming for himself the authority to ordain people as deacons and elders, and even as bishops! As Wesley himself knew well, the issue was not so straightforward. Wesley defended his actions by noting that he had not ordained anyone to do anything in any part of the world in which the Church of England was the established church. In an indirect way, the fact that the laypersons that Wesley ordained were never recognized as elders or deacons *in* the Church of England serves to support his point.

The most intriguing thing about Wesley's ordinations, however, is that scholars almost always see them primarily as raising questions about Wesley's disposition toward the Church of England. Very rarely are Wesley's ordinations seen as raising questions about the Church of England's disposition toward him. Yet surely Wesley's ordinations do raise at least one crucial question about the Church of England. If we assume that Wesley's life and ministry were following a trajectory of ever-increasing rebelliousness and disregard towards the established church, then why did the established church not regard his ordinations as the perfect excuse to revoke his orders or to excommunicate him entirely?

Once again, the secularization thesis holds considerable sway over our imaginations. On this thesis, as we have seen, the Church of England was simply too lax to pay attention to what its clergy were doing or to discipline them when they stepped out of line. Thus we are left to focus on what the ordinations tell us about Wesley's disposition toward the established church. However, if the Anglican stabilization thesis is correct, then the established church was not nearly as lax and indifferent as it has often been made out to have been. Thus we must provide a plausible explanation for why the church did not revoke Wesley's credentials or excommunicate him altogether.

One way to answer this question is simply to say that, from the standpoint of canon law, there was no case against Wesley. Wesley was correct in saying that he did not ordain anyone for ministry *in* the Church of England. However, in light of the Anglican stabilization thesis, we might add that the established church's failure to discipline Wesley reflects an ever-widening spirit of toleration. In other words, this may have reflected a disposition of generosity borne of a well-honed political strategy rather than a laxity borne of disempowerment or corruption. Whichever the case, Wesley's actions clearly did not lead either to the revocation of his credentials or to his excommunication from the Church of England. We will say more about this in a moment. For now, we need to take up a second issue; namely, the many criticisms aimed at Wesley by other Anglican clergy, most notably those aimed at him by his younger brother.

As we saw in Chapter One, Wesley spent a great deal of time and energy answering critics. In many cases, Wesley's critics questioned whether he was truly devoted to the established church. A good example of this are Thomas Church's letters to Wesley in the 1740s, to which Wesley responded with letters of his own, including the treatise 'The Principles of a Methodist Farther Explained' (1746). In this important work, Wesley devoted the lengthy third section to 'the point of Church communion', as pertaining to the Methodists' faithfulness or lack thereof to both the doctrine and the discipline of the Church of England.[69]

Many scholars take the fact that other Anglican clergy often questioned Wesley's loyalty to the Church of England as another sign that something was amiss. Yet there are at least three possible explanations for these criticisms of Wesley. While no one of them can alone explain the criticisms in their entirety, they might, when taken together, help to explain a large percentage of them.

First, there is the matter of territorialism among the clergy. In the eighteenth century, clergy were assigned to parishes, within which they had a certain amount of authority. When Wesley established a Methodist society in a parish, it is conceivable that the priest assigned to that parish perceived both Wesley and the society as a threat to his authority. In such cases, the easy thing to do was to bar Wesley from the pulpit and criticize his lack of respect for parish boundaries. At the same time, there were more than a few parish priests who welcomed Wesley in their pulpits and the Methodists in their services. Indeed, it is arguable that, were it not for the support of the clergy, the Methodist movement would never have made it off the ground.

Second, in not a few cases, the clergy who complained about Wesley and the Methodists may have been coerced into doing so by intolerant mobs. When we recall that the Methodists met with direct opposition from mobs on more than one occasion, this explanation for at least some of the criticism that Wesley received from clergy seems plausible.

Third, criticisms that do not reflect territorialism or coercion by mobs may reflect the work of constructing and maintaining a confessional state. In other words, it can be argued that public criticism of groups like the Methodists was a mechanism for sounding out extremism and for encouraging groups to remain in the broad channel of English church and society. Extending the metaphor, it is possible that queries about loyalty to the established church were the equivalent of well-timed and well-placed ecclesiastical buoys. If this is plausible, then the Methodists were exactly the sort of group for whose sake it would make sense for bishops and other high-ranking clergy to erect such buoys. Extreme groups like the Deists, Socinians and Catholics were simply (and repeatedly) torpedoed. By contrast, groups who had not already gone too far – groups like the Methodists – could be seen as simply needing occasional but unmistakable warnings about the ecclesiastical equivalent of shallow water.[70]

Wesley's relationship with one critic in particular deserves extended attention. As we saw in Chapter One, Charles Wesley frequently questioned his older brother's loyalty to the Church of England in the middle and later years of the revival. To date, the most influential thesis concerning Charles' criticism of John is that, by the later years of the revival, if not earlier, the brothers came to have significantly different priorities. Of course, the implication of this thesis is that Charles' criticisms were well-founded, that John's commitment to the established church was languishing. Thus Henry Rack says,

> In significant and total contrast with his brother . . . Charles declared that his 'chief concern on earth was the prosperity of the Church of England; my next, that of the Methodists; my third, that of the preachers': he would give them up for the sake of Methodism and the Methodists for the good of the church. Nothing could have been more subversive of John Wesley's sense of priorities or of what was needed to sustain his mission.[71]

At one level, Rack's interpretation appears to be spot-on, especially as it pertains to Charles. Thus it is widely agreed that Charles remained deeply committed to the Church of England. At another level, however, there may be a way to make a subtle but important conceptual distinction between 'priorities' and 'concerns' that provides a different angle from which to interpret what was going on here.

In everyday usage, the term 'priority' denotes a principled commitment. For example, if a person says 'x is a priority for me,' then we tend to assume that the person is more than casually committed to x. More important to notice is the fact that the concept of priority logically implies contrast. Thus people use the concept of priority in order to indicate the level of their commitment to one thing by comparison with their level of commitment to something else. This is especially the case with lists such as the ones with which we are working here. Consequently, to speak of priorities is to speak of an arrangement or ordering of commitments that, in most instances, reflects years of principled reflection and practice.

The concept of concern is different. In some cases, of course, the concept is used to denote a long-standing principled commitment.[72] However, in normal usage, people most often use the term 'concern' to indicate what they are worried about at a particular moment. For example, a person might say, 'I am concerned about my health,' or 'I am concerned about losing my job.' We can see, then, that in common usage, the concept of concern lacks the sense of long-term principled commitment. Conceptually, concern conveys worry about a present and temporal issue. Thus, in the example given above, if the person's health or sense of job security improves dramatically, then these things are no longer cause for concern. By contrast, priorities are not the sort of things that tend to come and go based on contingent realities. When someone says, 'You need to get your priorities straight,' the implication is that there is some agreed upon good or norm that is being ignored.

In order to see the relevance of this distinction for thinking about the difference between Charles' and John's loyalty to the Church of England, it is important to note that, while concerns tend to be more temporary than priorities, concerns can also temporarily relegate priorities to the background. For example, suppose my wife and children are considerably higher on my list of priorities than writing and publishing books. It is easy to imagine a situation in which my concern to meet a publishing deadline causes my prioritization of my wife and children temporarily to recede into the background. The fact that I devote more energy to writing for a few weeks or months at a time in order to meet a deadline does not mean that writing books has displaced my wife and children on my priority list.

For most people, it is acceptable for temporary concerns routinely to press long-haul priorities to the background precisely because they assume that the things at the top of their priority lists are more permanent. For example, people who put God at the top of their priority lists routinely assume that God is always there, that God will not suddenly cease to exist if they do not give God adequate attention in a particular week or even in a given month or year. Similarly, I assume that my wife and children will be waiting on me when I have met my deadline and therefore have more time for them.

This is a more nuanced way of thinking about what is going on with John Wesley's loyalty to the Church of England. It is possible that John and Charles actually had the exact same list of priorities. Indeed, unless we are prepared to press the claim that he was self-deceived or disingenuous, then John's repeated declarations of loyalty to the Church of England suggest the same list of priorities. Thus I suspect that John, no less than Charles, would readily sign on to an ordering of priorities as follows: God, the Church of England, the King, Methodism and the revival, the preachers, the poor and the well-being of English society. To be sure, he might want to tinker with the ordering of the bottom three, but I am relatively certain that he would leave the top four items exactly as they are.

The difference between the brothers may come down to John's sense of the constancy and stability of the Church of England over against his concern for the relative instability of the revival and the Methodist societies. Of course, the instability of the latter was only a deep concern because of the spiritual and physical needs of the people who were associated with the revival and the societies. Thus when it came to John and Charles' disagreement over the examination of the preachers, John's concern to cultivate their graces and gifts for ministry trumped any worry that the unlettered among them might somehow bring about the ruin of the Church of England. From John's point of view, the Church of England would be there no matter what. The fate of the preachers and of the people to whom they would minister was not nearly as certain.

Of course, the foregoing argument could be taken to mean that John Wesley simply took the Church of England for granted. More positively, one might say that Wesley trusted that the Church of England would be there, and with it the means of grace so vital to salvation. The Church of England was established. It was at the centre of English society in the eighteenth century. By contrast, the sort of folk that attended many of the Methodist societies had a far more spiritually and economically precarious existence. They were on the fringes of English church and society, and Wesley was determined to bring as much spiritual and economic stability to their lives as he could. Indeed, Wesley seems to have viewed himself as a special agent of the Church of England. Thus he once described his message and work as being for 'the lost sheep of the Church of England'.[73]

We have spent a great deal of time thinking about criticisms aimed *at* Wesley. It was also the case, however, that Wesley reserved his harshest criticisms for his fellow clergymen, referring to them as 'a stink in the nostrils of God'. What are we to make of such inflammatory rhetoric from the mouth of someone who claimed to be devoted to the Church of England? Two comments here will suffice.

First, it is important to pay attention to Wesley's audience, especially when his language is rhetorically severe. Wesley levied some of his harshest criticisms when he was writing to his critics, especially to critics whom he regarded as particularly obstinate or unfair. In such cases, Wesley routinely overstated his case in an attempt to make his position heard.

Second, the fact that Wesley was a harsh critic of the Church of England does not automatically mean that he was disloyal or that he did not love the church. As anyone who has ever been deeply devoted to an institution knows, those who are the most devoted are often precisely the ones who feel most compelled to criticize the institutions that they love, especially when they believe that those institutions can do better. In other words, harsh criticism can sometimes be a sign of depth of commitment rather than growing opposition.

That John Wesley professed to love the Church of England there can be no doubt. He said so plainly and frequently throughout the course of his life. Indeed, in his 'Reasons against a Separation from the Church of England' (1758), he referred to the established church affectionately as 'the mother of us all'. In the same treatise, he urged the Methodist preachers to be vigilant in attending the church, saying, 'And the more we attend it, the more we love it, as constant experience shows'.[74] Above all, the fact that Wesley made good on his promise to remain in the established church until he died suggests that his was the harsh criticism of a devoted son rather than a disaffected outsider.

The last form of evidence that scholars often cite to support the notion that Wesley was not deeply committed to the Church of England is his belief in miracles, the devil, demonic possession and the like. These beliefs routinely serve as evidence that Wesley was a reactionary figure who was deeply opposed to the increasingly secular nature of English church and society. However, in paying closer attention to what was actually the case on the ground, scholars have recently discovered that Wesley was by no means alone in believing in such things.[75] This is not to deny that some eighteenth-century English clergy did question miracles, the existence of the devil and demonic possession. Rather, it is simply to say that it is far from clear that the majority of clergy did so. Moreover, it is important to remember that people who question long-held beliefs often receive a disproportionate amount of attention from their contemporaries and from scholars. Thus there is a tendency to make David Hume the spokesperson for the status of belief in miracles in eighteenth-century England. In light of recent scholarship, it may be that it was Hume, and not Wesley, who was in the minority. Finally, we should be slow to assume that belief and disbelief in miracles, the devil, demon possession and the like can be charted according to a simple division between social and intellectual elites on the one hand and popular culture on the other. After all, when Conyers Middleton denied the continuation of miracles in the early church, it was not only John Wesley but also Bishop William Warburton who came to their defence.[76]

In assessing the major forms of evidence that scholars draw upon to show that Wesley was not as deeply committed to the established church as he claimed to be, we have seen two things clearly. On the one hand, we have seen that there is more than one way to interpret the evidence. In each case, there is a plausible way to interpret the evidence so that Wesley's actions do not contradict what he says about his devotion to the Church of England. On the other hand, we have seen that how we interpret the evidence depends to no small degree on our background assumptions about English church and society in the eighteenth century. To date, the majority of scholars have interpreted Wesley in the light of the secularization thesis. What would happen to our understanding of Wesley if we interpreted him in the light of the Anglican stabilization thesis instead? It is to this question that we now turn.

As suggested above, the work of constructing and maintaining a confessional state in the eighteenth century revolved around the development and deployment of a political theology that combined commitment to the Trinity and reception of the sacraments with a policy of toleration. In other words, representatives of the established church sought to unify and stabilize English society by keeping the list of essential orthodoxies as short as possible and by allowing room for innovation and diversity of opinion on non-essential matters. This combination of orthodoxy and generosity eliminated the most extreme positions, including Deism, Socinianism, Arianism and Catholicism, but it also allowed breathing room on many other fronts.

On this reading of the wider situation, one can argue that it was not out of mere laxity or indifference that episcopal leaders allowed Wesley to play fast and loose with Anglican sensibilities concerning clergy conduct. Rather, in light of their political theology, one can argue that they tolerated Wesley because he was precisely the kind of person for whom they were prepared to make room in English church and society. Wesley believed in the Trinity and he frequently partook of the sacraments. From the standpoint of the eighteenth-century Anglican hegemony, that was more than enough.

For his part, Wesley did not simply conform to the political theology of his day; he fully embraced it. Indeed, Wesley may be said to have represented eighteenth-century Anglican political theology as well as anyone. Thus, in addition to confessing the Trinity and frequently receiving the sacraments in the established church, Wesley did two things that reflect a strong commitment to the political theology of the established church. First, he firmly rejected groups that denied the Trinity or that downplayed the importance of receiving the sacraments in the established church. For example, after years of seeking their spiritual and theological council, Wesley severed his ties with the Moravians when they began to deny the importance of the sacraments for salvation. Similarly, he refused to offer a hand of fellowship to groups that denied the divinity of Christ, saying,

> And could any man answer these questions, – 'Dost thou believe in the Lord Jesus Christ, God over all, blessed for evermore?' (which, indeed, no Arian, semi-Arian, or Socinian can do) . . .; if, I say, any man could answer these questions in the affirmative, I would gladly give him my hand.[77]

Also worth noting here is the fact that Wesley specifically commissioned John Fletcher and then Joseph Benson to refute Joseph Priestley's Unitarian arguments for the mere humanity of Jesus. Given that he once told his preachers that they had 'nothing to do but to save souls', it is surely significant that Wesley asked two of his most trusted preachers to set aside time to address the leading anti-Trinitarian of his day.[78]

Second, Wesley worked to inscribe an Anglican political theology on the hearts and minds of his preachers and of the people called Methodists. For example, we can readily see both sides of this political theology on display in the treatise called 'The Character of a Methodist', in which Wesley says, 'We believe Christ to be the Eternal Supreme God; and herein we are distinguished from the Socinians and Arians. But as to all opinions which do not strike at the root of Christianity, we "think and let think".'[79] It is hard to imagine a more succinct and eloquent expression of eighteenth-century Anglican political theology.

Moreover, it is well-known that, while he experimented with a variety of religious practices within the societies, Wesley constantly admonished the Methodists to adhere closely to the doctrines of the Church of England and to receive the sacraments therein as often as they possibly could.[80] For that matter, he clearly believed that the doctrines and theology of the Methodists were the same as those of the Church of England. Thus, in 1761, Wesley urged James Knox 'steadily to adhere to *her* doctrine in every branch of it; particularly with respect to the two fundamental points, Justification by Faith and Holiness'.[81]

Ironically, the extent to which Wesley was concerned to inculcate in the Methodist movement a distinctively Anglican political theology is perhaps best demonstrated in the actions that he took with respect to the American Methodists in 1784. Unfortunately, this has often been obscured from sight by the scholarly obsession with Wesley's ordinations. America was no longer under the crown, and Wesley knew it. To the extent that church and crown went together in Wesley's mind (and the two most certainly did go together), this meant that the American Methodists were not officially

Anglican. Concerned that they would not have any fixed religious position, Wesley attempted to make them functionally Anglican by sending over revised editions of the Thirty-Nine Articles of Religion and the Prayer Book, the former insuring belief in the Trinity, the latter frequent reception of the sacraments. Suffice it to say, Wesley expected them to adhere closely to both.

Whether or not the American Methodists have ever taken these documents seriously is a matter of some scholarly debate, though many scholars conclude that they have not.[82] Whatever we make of this or of the eventual separation of the British Methodists from the Church of England, the fact remains that, by eighteenth-century standards, John Wesley was a representative Anglican. He was committed to the Trinity and the sacraments, and on the prevailing political theology of his day, this is what really mattered. Indeed, it appears that Wesley understood this better than most. Thus he declared,

Nothing can prove I am no *member* of the Church till I either am *excommunicated* or *renounce* her communion, and no longer join in her doctrine, and in the breaking of bread, and in prayer. Nor can anything prove, I am no *minister* of the Church, till I either am *deposed* from my ministry or *voluntarily renounce* her, and wholly cease to teach her doctrines, use her offices, and obey her rubrics for conscience' sake.[83]

CHAPTER THREE

HONOURING THE KING:
THE POLITICS OF DIVINE RIGHT

Above all, mark that man who talks of loving the Church, and does not love the King. If he does not love the King, he cannot love God.
John Wesley, 'A Word to a Freeholder'

One of the most perplexing things about John Wesley is the extent to which scholars are reluctant to take him at his word. For example, in the previous chapter, we noted that scholars claim that Wesley's declarations of allegiance to the Church of England cannot be taken at face value. Wesley's actions, we are told, consistently undermined his words.

Instinctively, it is hard to ignore such a claim. After all, conventional wisdom dictates that actions speak louder than words. Yet, by paying closer attention to the shape and direction of eighteenth-century English church and society, we were able to interpret Wesley's actions in a way that is more consistent with his unwavering claim to be a 'Church of England man'. More specifically, we were able to show that, in his commitment to the Trinity and sacraments, Wesley was a representative of the political theology of the established church. Accordingly, the established church allowed sufficient room for Wesley and the Methodist movement to flourish, though not without some occasional monitoring.

However, to substantiate our claim that Wesley was, by eighteenth-century standards, a representative Anglican, we will have to do more than simply observe that Wesley believed in the Trinity and frequently received the sacraments. After all, there were more than a few nonconformist groups who believed in the Trinity and in the sacraments. Moreover, by virtue of being nonconformists, such groups would have naturally been committed to toleration. Thus the fact that Wesley insisted that he and the Methodists believed in the divinity of Jesus Christ and the efficacy of the sacraments but otherwise preferred to 'think and let think' can just as easily be taken to support an argument that Wesley was a nonconformist who happened to believe in the Trinity, which is to say, that he was really a Puritan.[1]

If we are to show that Wesley was truly a representative Anglican, a member of the Anglican hegemony in the long eighteenth century, an establishment figure, and the like, then we must show that he was equally committed to the monarchy and to the politics of subordination as expressed in the ordering of English society. In other words, we must provide evidence that, like the architects of the confessional state, Wesley held to the Trinity and the sacraments not only for spiritual but also for political reasons. We know that Wesley had the right enemies (the Deists, Socinians, Arians and Catholics), but we need to know whether he opposed these groups not only on theological but also on political grounds.

Under most circumstances, the most straightforward way to determine a person's political disposition is to identify the political party to which a person belongs. From there, one can simply check to see whether a person's political commitments consistently reflect the commitments of the relevant party. Initially, this is precisely how scholars approached Wesley. In doing so, they generally took him at his word. Thus by the late nineteenth century, there was a standard portrait of Wesley's politics in place that was based on his claim to be a High Church Tory. Among other things, this claim was taken to mean that Wesley was a staunch supporter of the monarchy and of the principle of subordination in English society. Yet, just as scholars have called into question Wesley's repeated declarations of allegiance to the established church, they have also raised questions about Wesley's self-identification as a High Church Tory.

Once scholars questioned whether Wesley could be taken at his word when he said that he was a High Church Tory, an entire range of competing proposals emerged. Initially, there was no consensus about Wesley's political identity and principles. In recent years, however, a majority position has taken shape, according to which Wesley was, in his commitment to natural rights and human liberties, something approaching a proto-liberal democrat. This way of viewing Wesley's politics has been popular not just among scholars, but among present day American Methodists as well. It is not difficult to see why. The majority position brings Wesley closer to modern forms of Methodism, making him appear less stodgy and authoritarian, not to mention less aristocratic. More specifically, by making him more egalitarian, the majority view helps to bring Wesley in line with a prevailing myth about the egalitarianism of American Methodism.

Before we survey these scholarly developments related to Wesley's politics, we need to make sure that we see what is and what is not at stake here. What is not at stake here is whether or not Wesley's politics are compatible with our politics, or whether or not we can find common ground politically between Wesley and modern forms of Methodism. What is at stake here is the need to see Wesley whole. In other words, we need to see that

Wesley's political commitments support our reading of his ecclesiastical commitments. After that, we need to see that his theological commitments cohere with and support his ecclesiastical and his political commitments. For now, we need to examine Wesley's politics in the conventional sense of that term.

THE STANDARD PORTRAIT:
AN UNCHANGING HIGH CHURCH TORY

Through the first half of the twentieth century, historians would have been puzzled by the suggestion that there was anything perplexing about John Wesley's politics. Wesley's political identity was simply the sort of thing everyone knew. He was, by his own admission, a conservative High Church Tory.

Generally speaking, scholars during this period simply took Wesley at his word. For example, in what was among the most influential early twentieth-century monographs on Wesley's political philosophy, Maldwyn Edwards' *John Wesley and the Eighteenth Century* begins with the simple and straightforward declaration, 'John Wesley was a Tory.' Edwards quickly added that, throughout Wesley's life, 'his Toryism remained unchanged'.[2]

What, precisely, did Wesley's Toryism entail? What did it mean for Wesley to be a conservative High Church Tory? According to the standard portrait, High Church Tories believed in four basic things. First and foremost, they believed in the doctrine of divine right, which is to say, they believed that the monarch's power to rule derives directly and exclusively from God. Moreover, because they believed in the doctrine of divine right, they rejected the notion that the monarch's power to rule derives from the people or from Parliament.

Second, because they believed that the monarch's power to rule does not in any sense derive from the people, High Church Tories also believed that the people could have no hand in 'choosing' the monarch. In other words, High Church Tories believed in the doctrine of direct hereditary succession. Thus they rejected the Glorious Revolution and the Hanoverian succession as illegitimate. High Church Tories were, almost by definition, Jacobite sympathizers; they were hoping and perhaps even plotting for the return of James II and the Stuart line to the throne.

Third, because High Church Tories believed in the doctrine of divine right, they also believed in the doctrine of passive obedience or non-resistance. If the monarch's power to rule was derived from God, then it was incumbent upon the people to obey the monarch (or at least not to disobey the monarch) in all circumstances. Thus High Church Tories thought of themselves as loyal subjects, not citizens.

Finally, High Church Tories held to this network of political doctrines in part because they believed that the alternative was anarchy or mob rule.

Conservative High Church Tories were not unaware that monarchs could be unjust. They simply believed that the likelihood of order and stability was greater in a monarchy than it would be in a democracy.[3]

When early twentieth-century interpreters label Wesley a conservative High Church Tory, they are clearly thinking of the foregoing network of political commitments. For example, William Warren Sweet describes Wesley as a 'champion of order and the king' who, above all else, feared 'King mob'. Moreover, he says that Wesley was particularly 'undemocratic', contending that because God was the monarch's 'source of power', the people had 'no right to select their own rulers'.[4] On these grounds, Sweet concludes that Wesley was 'a staunch Tory in politics'.[5]

We can readily understand why early interpreters viewed Wesley the way they did. In addition to declaring himself a High Church Tory, Wesley made numerous comments throughout his life that would appear to reflect the network of High Church Tory views outlined above. For example, in 1744, Wesley affirmed that he and the Methodists 'earnestly exhort all with whom we converse, as they fear God, to honour the King'. Moreover, says Wesley, the Methodists urge all people 'to revere the higher powers' as being 'of God'.[6] In 1750, Wesley assured a local magistrate that 'I fear God and honour the king.'[7] In 1768, Wesley repeatedly voiced concern that, if people did not honour the present form of government, the result would be 'anarchy and confusion', the return of the violence of the Commonwealth, or the rule of 'king Mob'.[8] In 1772, Wesley insisted that the monarch's power to rule was 'derived from God, the Sovereign of all', and he explicitly condemned the notion that 'the people are the origin of power' as being in 'every way indefensible'.[9] Finally, in 1775, Wesley uttered what is perhaps his best known political remark, saying, 'I am an High Churchman, the son of an High Churchman, bred up from my childhood in the highest notions of passive obedience and non-resistance.'[10]

If there was a problem with the standard portrait, then it was not a lack of corroborating evidence in Wesley. Rather, from the standpoint of later scholarship, the problem was that advocates of the standard portrait were too selective. This, too, is understandable enough. Wesley's penchant for memorable turns of phrase made it all too easy for scholars to overlook more subtle but no less important themes.

Beginning in the 1970s, scholars began to observe that, alongside the evidence for the conservative High Church Tory doctrines outlined above, there was evidence of what appeared to be liberal, democratic or Whig sentiments in Wesley's political writings. Most notable here was Wesley's growing concern for natural rights and human liberty. Thus began the construction of an alternative portrait of Wesley's political identity. At the time, few people noticed that advocates of the standard portrait had assumed a rather narrow definition of Toryism. We will say more about this later. For now, we need to summarize the alternative portrait that emerged.

THE TWO-STAGE PORTRAIT: A WHIGGISH WESLEY?

If the standard portrait of Wesley's political identity was based on a rather narrow definition of Toryism in the eighteenth century, the discovery of a Whiggish Wesley was based on an equally narrow definition of eighteenth-century Whiggery. For example, Leon O. Hynson, following George Trevelyan, declared that Whigs were simply those people who were 'dedicated to guarantees of constitutional liberty'.[11] According to Bernard Semmel, Whigs favoured natural or human rights over the Tory doctrine of divine right.[12] They were therefore proponents of 'theories of social contract and popular sovereignty'.[13] By extension, whereas Tories opposed the American colonies' quest for independence, Whigs were 'sympathetic to the colonial cause'.[14] Applying these definitions to Wesley, Frederick Dreyer once quipped, 'If Wesley is a Tory in his denial of contract, in his assertion of natural liberty he is a Whig.'[15] The implication of this is clear. Tories were, by definition, opposed to natural rights and human liberties.

With this definition of Whiggery in hand, Hynson and Semmel challenged the standard view of Wesley as an unchanging High Church Tory. Independently of one another, they developed a two-stage theory, according to which the early or youthful John Wesley was a conservative High Church Tory. The later and more mature Wesley, by contrast, remained a Tory in his affirmation of divine right, but was otherwise quite Whiggish in his advocacy for natural rights and human liberty. Given the considerable influence of the two-stage theory in some quarters, it will help to examine it more closely.

Unlike some earlier interpreters, including the aforementioned William Warren Sweet and V. H. H. Green, Hynson and Semmel insisted that Wesley was, during his early years, not simply a Tory, but a Jacobite and Nonjuror as well.[16] For example, Semmel claimed that Wesley's 'early politics' were 'Tory and Jacobite', adding that, 'like his mentor William Law, he had even been a non-juror'.[17] Similarly, Hynson remarked that Wesley's nonjuror stage 'began at his mother's knee and continued . . . through the years of the nonjuring Holy Club' at Oxford.[18] Indeed, both Hynson and Semmel appealed almost exclusively to Wesley's upbringing by Samuel and Susanna Wesley and then to his education at Christ Church, Oxford to support their claims that the early Wesley was a Nonjuror and Jacobite. They provided no supporting quotations from Wesley himself.

The appeal to Wesley's upbringing must be taken seriously. As we saw in Chapter One, Wesley's mother, Susanna, was a Nonjuror in practice and a Jacobite in sentiment. Thus there is the notorious dispute between Samuel and Susanna Wesley that led initially to a period of separation and, ultimately, following reconciliation, to the conception and birth of John Wesley. As the oft-repeated story goes, Samuel Wesley was a supporter of the Glorious Revolution and the resulting Hanoverian line. By contrast, Susanna opposed the Revolution, refusing to swear an oath to William and Mary. One evening, this disagreement reached a climax when Susanna refused to say 'Amen' to Samuel's prayer for the king. When Samuel asked why she did not say 'Amen', Susanna replied that she 'did not believe the Prince of Orange was King'. In turn, Samuel said, 'If that be the case . . . you and I must part: for if we have two kings, we must have two beds.'[19] And part they did, with Samuel living in London for a time. Less than a year following Samuel's return home, John Wesley was born. There is no record of Susanna ever asking for forgiveness.

As this story illustrates, Wesley was born into a Tory family divided by the Glorious Revolution. On the one hand, Wesley's father and mother were committed High Church Tories, believing that the power to rule comes from God, not from any human person. Both Samuel and Susanna Wesley subscribed to the doctrines of divine right and passive obedience. On the other hand, Susanna believed that neither the people at large nor the Parliament had a right to displace the King from his throne. Thus she clearly adhered to the doctrine of direct or indefeasible hereditary right. In her judgement, William and Mary were illegitimate usurpers. Samuel differed from Susanna in that he accepted the Glorious Revolution and with it, by implication, the notion that Parliament could determine the succession of kings.

Like the appeal to his upbringing, the appeal to Wesley's student days at Oxford as evidence for his Jacobitism must be taken seriously. After all, there was no shortage of Nonjurors and Jacobites at Oxford in the 1720s, and it is well-known that Wesley associated with some of these individuals, including William Law and Thomas Deacon. According to one early twentieth-century interpreter of Wesley, these associates exercised considerable influence over Wesley, such that he 'took up a very definite position . . . in favor of the Stuarts'. The nonjuror climate at Oxford confirmed in Wesley's mind 'those sentiments which his mother had professed from the accession of William III'.[20]

At this point in the two-stage theory, Hynson discerned 'a transition period' during which Wesley began to disavow his earlier Jacobitism, gradually embracing a more Whiggish point of view. From 1734 to 1764, according to Hynson, Wesley replaced his commitments to divine right, indefeasible hereditary succession, passive obedience and non-resistance with a new set of commitments to limited monarchy and, most importantly, to human liberty and natural rights. This raises an obvious question: What caused Wesley to change his mind?

According to Hynson, the first and most important impetus for change came when Wesley read William Higden's *A View of the English Constitution*. Written in 1709, Higden's book was 'the work of a repentant non-juror', who was attempting 'to explain his reconciliation with the revolutionary monarchy of 1688–89'.[21] The upshot of the book's argument was that 'the supreme authority of the English government rests in the king . . . whether he was king de jure or de facto or both.' Moreover, Higden argued 'both from common law and from statute law', that subjects were obligated 'to obey the king in possession . . . because he is the only one to whom allegiance is due, according to the constitution'.[22]

On the strength of Higden's argument, says Hynson, Wesley 'became committed to the benefits of the limited monarchy'. To be sure, there were 'other recognizable factors' behind this change, but 'no other source' than Higden 'so clearly bridges the gulf between a rationale for divine right and belief in the limited monarchy'.[23] As we will see later, there is another way to understand Wesley's reaction to Higden.

For Semmel, it was not primarily Higden's work that led Wesley to change his mind. Rather, the primary catalyst for change was the repeated accusations that Wesley and the Methodists were Jacobites. On the eve of the '45 Rebellion, as fears grew that the Stuart Pretender would return to retake the throne by force, these accusations landed Methodist preachers, including Wesley himself, in the courts.[24] According to Semmel, it was primarily in an effort to secure ongoing toleration for the Methodist movement that Wesley rather conveniently 'began to preach absolute loyalty to George II'.[25]

Whatever combination of factors may have motivated Wesley to alter his politics in a Whiggish direction, Hynson and Semmel were in agreement that Wesley emerged from the 'transition period' a strong proponent of human liberty and natural rights. Thus both scholars called attention to the frequency with which Wesley emphasized these themes from 1768 to 1782, referring to this period as the 'second stage' in Wesley's political development. It was, after all, during this period that Wesley wrote and published all of his major political works, beginning with 'Free Thoughts on the Present State of Public Affairs' (1768) and concluding with the brief tract 'How Far is it the Duty of a Christian Minister to Preach Politics' (1782). All total, he wrote and published no less than 12 political essays during this time.[26]

Alongside affirmations of divine right and passive obedience, Wesley's political essays are, according to Hynson and Semmel, punctuated with Whiggish or liberal affirmations of human liberty and natural rights. For example, in the 1772 treatise 'Thoughts upon Liberty', Wesley describes liberty as the 'glory of rational beings and of Britons particularly'. Even more Whiggish are the repeated criticisms of previous English monarchs for their failure to provide for and protect the liberties of the people. For example, Wesley provides a rough-and-ready catalogue of the ways in which monarchs from Queen Mary to Charles II refused to grant their subjects the most basic of English liberties – namely, the liberties of conscience, property and goods.[27] Moreover, Wesley harshly criticizes the Act of Uniformity and the Act against Conventicles. Concerning the Act of Uniformity, he declares,

> So, by this glorious Act, thousands of men, guilty of no crime, nothing contrary either to justice, mercy, or truth, were stripped of all they had, of their houses, lands, revenues, and driven to seek where they could, or beg, their bread. For what? Because they did not dare to worship God according to other men's consciences! So they and their families were, at one stroke, turned out of house and home, and reduced to little less than beggary, for no other fault, real or pretended, but because they could not assent and consent to that manner of worship which their worthy governors prescribed![28]

Similarly, regarding the Act against Conventicles, he observes, 'Englishmen were not only spoiled of their goods, but denied even the use of the free air, yea, and the light of the sun, being thrust by hundreds into dark and loathsome prisons!'[29]

Even more important than the Whiggish criticism of previous monarchs is Wesley's anti-Jacobite insistence that it was only with the Glorious Revolution that England began truly to enjoy liberty. Thus in the 1777 treatise 'A Calm Address to the Inhabitants of England', he sternly advised, 'Never talk of the liberty of our forefathers: English liberty commenced at the Revolution.' Wesley quickly added that English liberty had reached a high point under George III, saying,

> And how entire is it at this day! Every man says what he will, writes what he will, prints what he will. Every man worships God, if he worships him at all, as he is persuaded in his own mind. Every man enjoys his own property; nor can the King himself take a shilling of it, but according to law. Every man enjoys the freedom of his person, unless the law of the land authorize his confinement. Above all, every man's life is secured, as well from the King, as from his fellow-subjects. So that it is impossible to conceive a fuller liberty than we enjoy, both as to religion, life, body, and goods.[30]

During this period, Wesley was also keenly interested in the American colonists' quest for liberty, about which he was both affirming and critical. For example, in the sentence immediately following the well-known remark about being 'an High Churchman, the son of an High Churchman, bred up from my childhood in the highest notions of passive obedience and non-resistance', Wesley goes on to say,

> And yet, in spite of all my rooted prejudice, I cannot avoid thinking (if I think at all) that an oppressed people asked for nothing more than their

legal rights, and that in the most modest and inoffensive manner which the nature of the thing would allow.[31]

At the same time, Wesley criticized the American colonists' quest for liberty as inconsistent and hypocritical, asking, 'Do not you observe, wherever these bawlers for liberty govern, there is the vilest slavery?'[32] Indeed, Wesley was particularly strong in his opposition to slavery in the name of human liberty and natural law. Thus in the 1774 treatise 'Thoughts Upon Slavery', he writes, 'I absolutely deny all slave-holding to be consistent with any degree of natural justice.'[33] He concluded the same treatise with the following appeal to natural law:

> Liberty is the right of every human creature, as soon as he breathes the vital air; and no human law can deprive him of that right which he derives from the law of nature.
> If, therefore, you have any regard to justice, (to say nothing of mercy, nor the revealed law of God,) render unto all their due. Give liberty to whom liberty is due, that is, to every child of man, to every partaker of human nature.[34]

As the foregoing examples demonstrates, Wesley was, in the political treatises of 1768–1782, a strong advocate for human liberties, including the liberties of conscience, free speech, property, freedom from bodily harm and the like. It is primarily on the basis of this emphasis on human liberty that Hynson and Semmel suggest that the later Wesley had moved in a decidedly Whiggish and liberal democratic direction. What are we to make of this proposal?

Soon after it emerged, scholars began to challenge crucial aspects of the two-stage theory. For example, numerous scholars called into question the claim that the early Wesley was a Nonjuror or Jacobite. On this front, they noted that, while the evidence that Samuel and Susanna Wesley differed considerably over the doctrine of direct hereditary right is quite strong, there is little, if any, evidence to support the claim that John Wesley sided with his mother. At best, such a judgement is based on the popular but largely unsubstantiated notion that Susanna was considerably more influential than Samuel in Wesley's early years.[35] The mere fact that Wesley encountered Nonjuror and Jacobite sentiments in the person of his mother does not mean that he adopted those sentiments for himself. On the contrary, the most that can be said with certainty is that, when he left home for Charterhouse school and ultimately for Oxford, Wesley was, like both of his parents, a High Church Tory committed to the doctrines of divine right and passive obedience (the very thing he claimed for himself many years later). It is far from clear whether, like his mother, he also subscribed to the doctrine of indefeasible hereditary right.

If the early Wesley was not a Nonjuror or a Jacobite, then the degree of difference between the early and the later Wesley is considerably diminished. Indeed, even Hynson and Semmel readily admitted that the later Wesley continued to subscribe to the most basic of Tory doctrines – namely, the doctrines of divine right and nonpassive resistance. Nor is it clear, as we will see below, that a person holding these doctrines could not affirm human liberties. For now, we need briefly to examine an even deeper problem with the two-stage portrait.

When considering Wesley's political identity, it is very important to pay close attention to the wider political landscape of eighteenth-century England. That landscape, as things turn out, exhibits an increasing overlap between the political commitments of Whigs and Tories, conservatives and liberal democrats and the like. Thus Frank O'Gorman observes that there is a real difficulty with using the labels 'Tory' and 'Conservative' to describe persons in the early and mid-eighteenth century. This difficulty stems from the fact that 'such unmistakably "Tory" or "Conservative" values as the defence of authority, the continuity of institutions, the rights of property and the rule of law . . . were so widespread that the terms become almost meaningless'.[36] In other words, party identities in the eighteenth century were more fluid than most textbook definitions would suggest.

As it happens, we do not have to look further than Wesley himself to see the changing nature of party identities. While clues are abundant in Wesley's political writings, one example will suffice to make the point. In 1768, Wesley addressed the growing agitation over John Wilkes' (1725–1797) election to Parliament from Middlesex, an election overturned by the House of Commons. Wilkes and his supporters argued that Parliament should not have the power to overturn the decision of the electorate. For his part, Wesley believed the House of Commons had done the right thing, seeing him as a profligate unfit for a seat in Parliament. What really seems to have bothered Wesley, however, was the extent to which the growing controversy threatened to divide and destabilize the country. Thus, in the treatise 'Free Thoughts on the Present State of Public Affairs', Wesley lamented regarding the controversy,

> The flame spreads wider and wider; it runs as fire among the stubble. The madness becomes epidemic, and no medicine hitherto has availed against it. The whole nation sees the State in danger, as they did the Church sixty years ago; and the world now wonders after Mr. Wilkes, as it did then after Dr. Sacheverel.[37]

Early interpreters of Wesley's political identity took this statement as evidence that Wesley was a conservative, High Church Tory. This is an understandable inference to the extent that textbook definitions of Tory politics indicate that Tories were committed to divine right and passive obedience, in part because they were convinced that it was the best way to avoid anarchy. However, such a reading focuses too much on the mobs chanting Wilkes' name, overlooking the fact that Wesley is comparing Wilkes' supporters with those who had been followers of Dr Sacheverell.

David Hempton is among the few commentators to notice that there is something other than politics-as-usual going on here. With characteristic understatement, Hempton observes, 'Anyone who could speak of Sacheverell and Wilkes in the same breath was certainly not a Tory of the old school.'[38] As the phrase 'old school' indicates, the inference to be drawn from this passage in Wesley is not that he had left Toryism for Whiggery, but that the Tory party itself had undergone extensive change. Had Wesley been a Tory of the 'old school', he could not have suggested that the dangers associated with Wilkes were akin to the dangers associated with Dr Sacheverell. After all, Wilkes was about as far removed from old school Toryism as one could get, while Dr Sacheverell had a cult following among the old school Tories.

We can now see that the deeper problem with the two-stage portrait of Wesley is that it fails to pay attention to the shifting identity of eighteenth-century Toryism. As Harry L. Howard observes,

> The error of Hynson's position is that it defines 'Tory' in terms that were fifty years too late, and even then it fails to account for the diversity of thought within the Tory camp in the late seventeenth and early eighteenth centuries.

Howard continues, 'What happened in the years of the eighteenth century was that Toryism underwent a transformation that, in many respects, left it looking similar to the old Whig party of the Glorious Revolution.' Thus Wesley's commitment to human liberty does not necessarily constitute a second Whiggish stage. Rather, it may simply reflect Toryism as it existed in the mid- to late eighteenth century. Similarly, Wesley's acceptance of the Hanoverian dynasty does not necessarily entail a move away from Toryism, as many Tories were among the architects of the Glorious Revolution. Indeed, as evidenced by their support for the Act of Settlement, not a few eighteenth-century Tories moderated or even abandoned their commitment to the absolute divine right of kings.[39]

If the shifting nature of party identities in the eighteenth century presents a deep challenge for the two-stage theory, then it should also serve as a warning for all future commentators on Wesley's political identity. As David Hempton observes, 'Putting labels on Wesley's political theology, whether Tory, Whig, mainstream Anglican, conservative, progressive or whatever, ultimately conceals as much as it reveals.'[40] How, then, should we proceed?

One possible way forward is initially to bracket the concern about party labels and to refocus our attention on Wesley's specific political commitments, including his commitments to divine right and passive obedience, to human liberty, to King, constitution and Parliament, to rank and order in society and the like. If the combination of Wesley's specific political commitments do not fit our preconceived notions of the Tory party, then we will have to decide which of our views to change. We can either alter our view of Wesley's political identity, or we can make adjustments to our view of the Tory party. To date, the former strategy has generated far more confusion and disagreement than consensus. By contrast, the latter strategy coheres well with a growing scholarly consensus that eighteenth-century English Toryism was dynamic and complex rather than static and monolithic.

The problem with this approach is that, in order to be taken seriously, it will have to be accompanied by a consideration of the political commitments of a wide range of people who self-identified as Tories. In other words, any attempt to reconstruct the meaning of political terms in the context of the eighteenth century from particular cases cannot rest on the political commitments of John Wesley alone, even though he certainly deserves to be on the list of cases to be considered.[41] Needless to say, the consideration of such a wide range of particular cases is a project that will take years, if not decades, to complete.

Until someone conducts a thorough assessment of Tory identity in the eighteenth century, another way forward is possible. Instead of focusing on the relationship between Wesley's political commitments and his Tory identity, we can inquire after Wesley's political philosophy. More specifically, we can inquire after the ordering of Wesley's political principles. On this approach, our goal will be to determine which political principle, if any, governed Wesley's political outlook and decision making.

This second approach is the one taken by several recent interpreters of Wesley's political views. Among the most notable to do so is the aforementioned David Hempton. This hardly comes as a surprise. After all, Hempton is clearly nervous about any attempt to attach party labels to Wesley's politics. Another prominent interpreter to take this approach is Theodore W. Jennings. As we will see, Jennings' motivation for inquiring after Wesley's political principles appears to differ considerably from Hempton's. It is to these two interpreters and the shift of emphasis from Wesley's political party to his political principles that we now turn.

WESLEY'S POLITICAL PRINCIPLES: TWO RECENT PORTRAITS

In some ways, David Hempton's portrayal of Wesley's politics differs markedly from Semmel and Hynson's two-stage theory. For example, Hempton has serious reservations about any claim that Wesley was ever a Nonjuror and a Jacobite. For that matter, as we have seen, Hempton is more reluctant than either Semmel or Hynson to label Wesley as conservative or liberal, as a Tory or a Whig.

In other ways, however, Hempton's portrait is similar to the two-stage thesis. Thus, while denying that Wesley was actually a Jacobite, Hempton agrees with Semmel's suggestion that Wesley became more vocal in his support of the Hanoverian dynasty in order to safeguard the Methodist movement from accusations of Jacobitism. Thus Hempton says that, 'after Wesley launched his religious movement in the late 1730s', he recognized that 'support for the king offered a more realistic prospect of securing basic toleration than would ever have been delivered by the old Laudian High Churchmen who hated the revival with a consuming passion.'[42]

The really pivotal move in Hempton's portrait, however, is his claim that Wesley's support for the Hanoverian dynasty was only partly motivated by his concern to protect the upstart Methodist movement. Indeed, it is precisely here that Hempton turns his attention from Wesley's party identity to his political principles. Thus he contends that Wesley's support for the Hanoverians was ultimately a reflection of his principled commitment to natural rights and human liberty and his 'settled conviction that the Glorious Revolution had ushered in an unprecedented era of civil and religious liberty in British society'.[43] To be sure, says Hempton, Wesley believed that God was 'the origin of all power'. Moreover, he clearly loved 'his king, his country and the constitution'. Above these, however, was Wesley's 'exalted view of civil and religious liberty which he sought to defend against violence and anarchy'. Thus Hempton contends that Wesley's approval of political events and outcomes 'went only to changes that in his opinion resulted in more, not less, civil and religious liberty'.[44]

One problem with Hempton's portrait is that all of the evidence that he cites comes from Wesley's political writings between 1768 and 1782. Yet, as we have seen, Wesley's public support for the Hanoverian dynasty preceded this period by almost 30 years. This does not mean, of course, that Wesley's initial support for the Hanoverian dynasty was not primarily the result of a principled commitment to liberty rather than a prior commitment to the doctrine of divine right *sans* the doctrine of indefeasible hereditary succession (confirmed by his reading of Higden) or of a pragmatic impulse to secure ongoing toleration for Methodists. Rather, it simply means that, apart from evidence that Wesley appealed to a principle of human liberty and natural rights in the late 1730s and 1740s, Hempton's portrait is fuzzy at best, accounting for Wesley's Hanoverian Toryism on the basis of materials written and published 30 years after he first pledged his support for the House of Hanover.

Before we raise any additional concerns about Hempton's portrayal of Wesley's politics, we should note that Hempton is by no means alone either in his turn to political principles or in his judgement that a principle of natural rights and human liberties governed Wesley's political outlook and decision making. Indeed, there is now something approaching a scholarly consensus that Wesley's politics did indeed revolve around a principled commitment to natural rights and human liberties. Interestingly enough, this consensus is made up of scholars who regard Wesley as a forerunner of liberal democracy and scholars who regard him as a proto-Marxist liberation theologian.

Of the latter group, Theodore W. Jennings is easily the most influential commentator on Wesley's politics. In the main, Jennings' approach to and conclusions about Wesley's politics are almost identical with Hempton's. Like Hempton, Jennings clearly wants to avoid making any strong judgements about Wesley's relationship to political parties in order to focus on Wesley's political principles. Also like Hempton, Jennings insists that human liberty and natural rights were 'the decisive norm' for Wesley's 'political ethic'.[45] Finally, like Hempton, Jennings maintains that Wesley's commitment to the monarchy and to the politics of subordination was motivated by pragmatic considerations having to do with the maintenance of good legal standing for the Methodists. Indeed, Jennings goes so far as to say that Wesley simply 'used' the monarchy for his own ends.

At this stage, three observations about what is happening here are in order. First, despite some differences with the two-stage portrait, there is also a direct line of continuity between Semmel and Hynson on the one hand, and Hempton and Jennings on the other. In all four of these interpreters, the heaviest emphasis by far is on Wesley's concern for natural rights and human liberties.

Second, the emphasis on Wesley's concern for natural rights and human liberties lines up nicely with the dominant line of interpretation concerning the early success of American Methodism. Beginning with the work of Nathan O. Hatch and continuing in the work of John H. Wigger and others, historians of religion in America have with increasing frequency portrayed Methodism as tailor-made for an emerging American liberal democratic ideology of structural egalitarianism with its promise of upward social and economic mobility.[46] For American Methodists who think of their tradition in these terms and who are eager to trace their history to Wesley, the image of Wesley as a proto-liberal democrat has been irresistibly enticing.[47]

Third, as we have seen in the work of Jennings, not all scholars who emphasize Wesley's concern for natural rights and human liberties do so in order to argue that Wesley is among the forerunners of liberal democracy. On the contrary, many Methodist theologians see in Wesley a forerunner of a Marxist-inspired liberationist politics. Indeed, Jennings himself finds in Wesley's commitment to natural rights and human liberties the grounds for suspicion not only of constitutional monarchies but of liberal democracies as well. Thus, he says,

A Wesleyan political ethic may find ample room for development here. But it also has the added precedent of Wesley's 'hermeneutic of suspicion', directed against those who use talk of liberty as a cover for the promotion of special and limited interests, who use talk of democracy as a cover for avarice and arrogance. The spiritual descendents of slaveholders and merchant princes of Wesley's day have often acted in ways that have left many in the Third World more than a little dubious about the motives of those who promote 'liberal democracy' or even 'democratic capitalism'. They may find that Wesley is a useful example of the sort of critique that may also be relevant today.[48]

With such a broad appeal, it is tempting to think that this view of Wesley's politics is the correct one. Surely it says something that liberal democrats and those with a Marxist orientation are in agreement here. But that is not the case. Rather, the fact that liberal democrats and those with a Marxist orientation are drawn to this way of portraying Wesley's politics turns out to be cause for suspicion. After all, there is more than a material similarity here. There is also a similarity in outcome, if not in aim. Whether or not this way of reading Wesley's politics is driven by a desire to bring Wesley closer to us will have to be discerned on a case-by-case basis. For example, while Jennings' search for Wesley's political principles is clearly driven by such a desire, the motivations for Hempton's work are less clear. What is not debated is that the emphasis on Wesley's concern for natural rights and human liberties makes Wesley sound more like he belongs to the twentieth or twenty-first century rather than to the eighteenth.

The problem here is not that natural rights theory is a twentieth-century phenomenon. In point of fact, natural rights theory predates the eighteenth century by quite a while. Rather, the problem lies in making the concern for natural rights and human liberty the 'norm' for Wesley's political outlook and decision making. It is one thing to note that Wesley valued natural rights and human liberties. It is another thing altogether to maintain that this was Wesley's most deeply held political principle, on the basis of which he determined whether to support the Hanoverian monarchy, whether to give money to the poor, and the like. This was simply not the case. Indeed, the majority view stands Wesley's political principles on their head.

The Politics of Divine Right: Obedience and Liberty

In the wake of a growing consensus that natural rights and human liberty constitute the deep ground or norm for Wesley's politics, Theodore R. Weber issued a rejoinder that, from the time of its publication until now, has remained a much neglected minority report.[49] Over against the majority view, Weber depicted Wesley as an 'organic constitutionalist'. In doing so, he was not simply returning to the standard portrait of Wesley as a High Church Tory. Weber's work is much more sophisticated and nuanced than that.

Unique to Weber's portrait is his insistence that Wesley was a constitutionalist. More than any interpreter before him, Weber has picked up on the fact that Wesley affirmed the ancient constitution with 'its reciprocating institutions of king, Lords, and Commons; its embedded historic rights; and its supporting and confirming traditions'. More specifically, says Weber, Wesley affirmed

> the particular constitutional settlement of 1689, which retained the prominence of the king but without the Tory ideology that absolutized his power, demoted Parliament to an advisory body, and considered the king superior to the law (because he was the source of the law).[50]

Wesley's occasional references to the constitution confirm this aspect of Weber's portrait. For example, in a sermon written in 1741, Wesley says that he has 'a zealous regard for the constitution we have received from our fathers'.[51] Similarly, in 'The Doctrine of Original Sin', an essay written in 1756, Wesley declares, 'We are under an excellent constitution, which secures both our religious and civil liberty.'[52] Lastly, there is this quotation attributed to Wesley in 1790 by the *Leeds Intelligencer*: 'That if the best of Kings – the most virtuous of Queens – and the most perfect constitution, could make any nation happy, the people of this country had every reason to think themselves so.'[53]

Equally important is Weber's designation of Wesley's political philosophy as 'organic'. According to Weber, Wesley 'believed that England was a unity of king (constitutional monarchy, which included Parliament), church, and people'. Moreover, Wesley's organicism 'placed him in a political tradition running from Richard Hooker to Edmund Burke, and therefore not in the tradition of individualistic liberalism'.[54]

Here, too, Wesley himself can be shown to support Weber's reading. For example, we can see the organic nature of Wesley's political philosophy when, in 'A Word to a Freeholder' (1747), he advises his readers on how to vote in an upcoming election, saying,

> Above all, mark that man who talks of loving the Church, and does not love the King. If he does not love the King, he cannot love God. And if he does not love God, he cannot love the Church. He loves the Church and the King just alike. For indeed he loves neither one nor the other.
>
> O beware, you who truly love the Church, and therefore cannot but love the King; beware of dividing the King and the Church, any more than the King and country. Let others do as they will, what is that to you? Act you as an honest man, a loyal subject, a true Englishman, a lover of the country, a lover of the Church; in one word, a Christian![55]

Now that we have a better sense for what Weber means when he says that Wesley was an 'organic constitutionalist', we need to see why this undermines the majority view that natural rights and human liberties were the norm for Wesley's politics. To be sure, Weber affirms that 'natural rights (read later as *human* rights) played a role – and an important one – in Wesley's political thinking.' Yet this does not mean that he agrees with the majority view. The question at hand is not whether Wesley was an advocate for natural rights and human liberties, but whether a principle of natural rights was 'determinative of his political thinking' to the extent that Semmel, Hynson, Jennings and Hempton contend that it was.[56] This Weber denies for the following four reasons.

First, Weber notes that the notion that Wesley derived his doctrine of rights and liberty from 'original nature as created by God' is central to the argument that he is a natural rights thinker.[57] Upon closer inspection, however, Weber shows that, in his doctrine of creation and nature, Wesley speaks primarily, if not exclusively, of liberty, not rights. For example, in describing the natural image of God in which man [*sic*] was created, Wesley says,

> He was, after the likeness of his Creator, endued with *understanding*, a capacity for apprehending whatever objects were brought before it, and of judging concerning them. He was endued with a *will*, exerting itself in various affections and passions; and, lastly, with *liberty*, or freedom of choice, without which all the rest would have been in vain, and he would have been no more capable of serving his Creator than a piece of earth or marble. He would have been as incapable of vice or virtue as any part of the inanimate creation. In these, in the power of self-motion, understanding, will, and liberty, the natural image of God consisted.[58]

The most important thing to notice here is that liberty has to do with the exercise of the will in obedience or disobedience to the moral law of God. As such, says Weber, the crucial issue is 'not right, but responsibility'. With respect to original nature as created by God, liberty's 'first order of business is obeying and loving God, not defining rights and claiming them'.[59]

As things turn out, human individuals do not get to exercise their wills responsibly for very long. With the fall into sin, the natural liberty with which God endowed humankind at creation disappears, replaced by the bondage of the will. Human individuals are now incapable of loving and obeying God naturally, that is, in a state of nature. Rather, from this point forward, loving and obeying God will depend on the transformation of the will and of human desire by God's grace.[60] Thus, if natural rights and liberties refer to the rights and liberties given to human individuals by God in their natural created state and subsequently obliterated by sin, then it does not make sense to say that natural rights and liberties are the norm for Wesley's politics.

The second reason that Weber denies that natural rights and liberties are the principle or norm of Wesley's politics has to do with Wesley's discussion of civil and religious liberties rather than with the natural liberty of the original created order. For Wesley, civil and religious liberties have to do with 'protections provided to individuals by the constitutional, governmental, and legal structure of a particular country'.[61] Suffice it to say, these are the 'natural' rights and liberties that Semmel, Hynson, Hempton and Jennings have in mind, despite the fact that, for Wesley, they are clearly a product of the contingent social and political arrangements after the fall. They are not truly 'natural' rights and liberties 'of human beings as such', but the 'rights of the people of England'. They are, as Weber puts it, 'Edmund Burke's *Rights of Englishmen*, not Thomas Paine's *Rights of Man*'.[62]

To the casual observer, this last point may seem like a matter of semantics. It is not. From Wesley's point of view, to acknowledge that civil and religious liberties are liberties of a contingent historical and social nature makes all the difference in the world. It means, among other things, that they are granted by a sovereign to whom people are subject and therefore to whom they owe obedience in exchange for their privileges. Thus, in addressing the American colonists' arguments for natural liberties, Wesley says,

> But you say, you 'are entitled to life, liberty, and property by nature; and that you have never ceded to any sovereign power the right to dispose of these without your consent'.
>
> While you speak as the naked sons of nature, this is certainly true. But you presently declare, 'Our ancestors, at the time they settled these colonies, were entitled to all the rights of natural-born subjects within the realm of England.' This likewise is true; *but when this is granted, the boast of original rights is at an end*. You are no longer in a state of nature, but sink down into colonists, governed by a charter. If your ancestors were subjects, they acknowledged a Sovereign; if they had a right to English privileges, they were accountable to English laws, and had ceded to the King and Parliament the power of disposing, without their consent, of both their lives, liberties, and properties. And did the Parliament cede to them a dispensation from the obedience which they owe as natural subjects? or any degree of independence, not enjoyed by other Englishmen?[63]

It is interesting to note that, as with the liberty that belonged to the natural image of God bestowed upon humankind in creation (and subsequently lost through the fall), civil and religious liberties are here intimately connected with obedience. In the first instance, God bestowed the liberty of the natural image upon humankind so that people would be capable of obeying and loving God freely. In the second instance, the price that one must pay for the religious and civil liberties provided by a sovereign is obedience. Moreover, just as failure to obey God resulted in the loss of liberty, it is obvious from the above quotation that Wesley believed that failure to obey a political sovereign would also result in a forfeiture of civil and religious liberties. Thus it is fair to say that, while the initial provision of liberty is a matter of the sheer gratuity and generosity of either God or a political sovereign, maintaining that liberty is dependent upon the recipient's ongoing obedience. At best, then, Wesley's norm for political ethics is a combination of liberty and obedience, although it is looking increasingly as though obedience trumps liberty and rights. After all, a failure to obey warrants the loss of liberties and rights.

Weber's third reason for denying that liberty or rights is the norm for Wesley's politics picks up where the second reason left off – namely, with an observation about the nature of sovereignty. If we look back at the excerpt from Wesley's letter to the American colonists, we can see that, in point of fact, Wesley believed that the sovereign was within his or her rights to revoke rights and privileges at any time, including the most basic civil and religious liberties. Such is the nature and meaning of sovereignty. Thus Weber says, 'The clearest evidence that John Wesley was not a consistent human rights or natural rights thinker is that he rejected the concept of political rights in any listing of civil liberties.' Weber continues,

> In political society, according to Wesley, the concept of *right* belongs in essence to the supreme power, not to the members of society. . . . The people have no right at all to be represented in the deliberations and decisions of the government, and no inherent right to vote in the election of those who deliberate and decide. Moreover, they have no right to be free of the command and control of the government, that is, no right to independence. However, they do have a clear *duty* to obey those who – under God – are set in authority over them.[64]

At the end of this summary of Wesley's view of the nature and power of political sovereigns we can discern Weber's fourth reason for denying that a principle of natural rights was the norm for Wesley's politics, namely, the fact that the sovereign's power derives directly from God. As things turn out, Wesley took the doctrine of divine right much more seriously that many interpreters want to admit. Thus Weber concludes,

> John Wesley's deliberate and vigorous exclusion of natural rights from the political process is not the only barrier to portraying him as a human rights thinker. Another barrier is that the basic principle of his political ethic is duty, not individual rights. Wesley's political-moral doctrine begins with the notion of the existent supreme power, which, by reason

of its supremacy in the political society, receives divine ordination to exercise the power under God. This notion of divine ordination entails the duty of subjects to obey those who are set in authority over them, with the understanding that they are obeying persons who stand in the place of God.[65]

What, then, does Weber make of the specific occasions on which Wesley clearly invokes the concept of natural rights and liberties? There are at least three such occasions, including his arguments against slavery, his arguments for the equality and natural rights of women, and his arguments for religious liberty or liberty of conscience. In the interest of fairness to the majority view, we should take a moment to summarize Weber's analysis of the arguments that Wesley deployed on each of these occasions. As we go, the thing to notice is that, on Weber's view, Wesley deployed the concept of natural rights 'to apply to conditions *within society*' rather than to suggest that natural rights were a matter of 'political rights of consent and self-governance in a presocial state of nature'.[66] This distinction is of vital importance, insofar as it marks the difference between Wesley's views and modern liberal democratic politics. Unlike much modern liberal democratic political philosophy, Wesley never thinks of natural rights outside the context of pre-existing political structures, laws, and the like. Thus Weber says, 'One does not grasp the meaning of rights and liberties for Wesley without perceiving that he views them in the mesh of institutions and traditions.'[67]

One specific occasion on which Wesley appeals to natural rights is in his arguments against slavery. Here, Weber readily concedes that the concept of natural rights plays a critical role in Wesley's argument. However, he astutely notes that Wesley frames the issue in terms of a problem with English law. Under English law, the colonists have a right not to be 'owned and controlled'. Unfortunately, the law 'does not offer the same protection to enslaved Africans'.[68] Thus even in the context of his arguments against slavery, Wesley thinks of rights and liberties as the sort of things that are bestowed by existing governments with the reciprocal requirement that obedience to the law follow.

A second occasion has to do with Wesley's arguments for the equality and rights of women. Here we are dealing with what seems to be an exception. Thus Wesley makes a clear argument from natural rights in favour of women being able to visit the sick. More specifically, Wesley makes the case on the basis of women being 'rational creatures' who, no less than men, are 'made in the image of God'.[69] Thus the appeal is to that part of the natural image that was not obliterated by sin, namely, rationality. Of course, Wesley could have noted that those aspects of the natural image that were decimated by sin, most notably the freedom of the will, apply equally to men and women. Unfortunately, as Weber notes, the appeal to natural rights in this case does not extend very far. For example, when it came to the question of whether women could preach, Wesley appealed to Scripture rather than natural rights, denying that it was permissible. Nor was Wesley willing to extend the argument to the political author-ization of women within the Methodist conference. These things combine to show that 'natural right was not a norm ultimately decisive' for Wesley with regard to making determinations about what women could and could not do.[70]

A third and final occasion on which Wesley deployed the concept of nat-ural rights was in arguments concerning religious liberty, or what he often called 'the rights of conscience'. Indeed, it is in this area that Wesley most frequently appealed to the notion of rights. For example, in a very import-ant passage in 'Thoughts Upon Liberty', Wesley says,

> Religious liberty is a liberty to choose our own religion, to worship God according to our own conscience, according to the best light we have. Every man living, as man, has a right to this, as he is a rational creature. The Creator gave him this right when he endowed him with understanding. And every man must judge for himself, because every man must give an account of himself to God. Consequently, this is an indefeasible right; it is inseparable from humanity. And God did never give authority to any man, or any number of men, to deprive any child of man thereof, under any colour or pretence whatever. What an amazing thing is it, then, that the governing part of almost every nation under heaven should have taken upon them, in all ages, to rob all under their power of this liberty! yea, should take upon them, at this day, so to do; to force rational creatures into their own religion![71]

Commenting on this passage, Weber says, 'This statement is an unambigu-ous declaration of natural right.' Yet Weber notes that 'what makes reli-gious liberty a natural *right*' is not 'the sanctity of rational freedom itself but what it implies for a person's relationship to God'. Weber continues,

> Wesley does not mean to suggest that choosing one's religion is a matter of indifference – of going down the cafeteria line until we find some-thing we like, or perhaps choosing nothing at all. It is not a liberal 'free-dom of choice' plan. Rather, it is a responsibility of ultimate seriousness in which everyone must give an account of himself or herself to God. No one else can fulfill that grave responsibility for another, and no one should attempt or be allowed to do so. Coercing another person's reli-gious belief is more than the violation of a right; it is a usurpation of the responsibility for one's own eternal destiny. . . . The true location of the right [to religious liberty] is in the divine-human relationship, not in human reason apart from God.[72]

There is a great deal more that could be said here. However, the most important thing to note may be the fact that, as in the case with women, there were clear limits as to how far Wesley was willing to extend his appeal. Contrary to popular and scholarly perceptions (particularly among American Methodists who routinely hold up Wesley's 'Letter to a Roman Catholic' as evidence that Wesley was at least ecumenical, if not pro-Catholic), Wesley had strong anti-Catholic sentiments.[73] Most notable here is his 'late-in-life objection to removing legal restrictions on Roman Catholics'.[74] The specific occasion for this objection was the passing of the Catholic Relief Act in 1778. From Wesley's point of view, Catholics could not be trusted to obey the British government because they had sworn a prior oath of allegiance to the Pope. Thus he says,

> But as long as it is so, nothing can be more plain than that the members of that Church can give no reasonable security to any Government of their allegiance or peaceable behavior. Therefore they ought not to be tolerated by any Government, Protestant, Mahometan, or Pagan.[75]

This is a striking remark. Indeed, it should have the effect of jarring us awake from the daydream that Wesley was a modern liberal democratic thinker or that he viewed England in increasingly modern liberal democratic terms. The clear implication in Wesley's argument against toleration for Catholics is that England was a decidedly Protestant confessional state. Otherwise, he would not have been so adamant that Catholics could not be trusted to obey the British government. From Wesley's perspective, Protestantism was as endemic to eighteenth-century England as Islam was to eighteenth-century Persia (modern-day Iran).

POLITICS AND THEOLOGY DISJOINED:
A CHARGE OF INCONSISTENCY

Among the few scholars to pay close attention to Weber's thesis, D. Stephen Long is exactly right in his assessment of Weber's contribution to our view of Wesley's political identity and principles when he says, 'After Weber's convincing analysis of Wesley's understanding of rights and liberties, it will be difficult to see how anyone can read him as a protomodern.'[76] Indeed, Weber's portrayal of Wesley as an organic constitutionalist supports our contention in Chapter Two that Wesley was a strong supporter of the confessional state in the long eighteenth century. After all, he not only insisted on belief in the Trinity and frequent reception of the sacraments, but he also insisted on obedience to the King and to English law. Thus it is plausible to argue that Wesley's commitment to the Trinity and sacraments was simultaneously an ecclesial, a political and a theological commitment. Or was it?

Interestingly enough, Weber himself maintains that, while Wesley's politics were in line with High Church Anglicanism, there was a deep incoherence between his politics and his theology. This incoherence, he claims, was twofold. First, according to Weber, Wesley's doctrine of God did not cohere well with his politics. Thus, he says, 'The God of Wesley's politics is a hierarchical first person of the Trinity – above us, judging, dispensing, disposing.'[77] As such, it was a mismatch for Wesley's constitutionalism. Weber continues,

> A hierarchical theology of politics that ordains the peak of power in society with supreme authority does not cohere with a political system designed to control dominant power and diversify authority, that is to say, a constitutional system. If constitutionalism is to be interpreted in theological terms, the theology cannot be simply hierarchical. It must begin to derive authority from below, not only from above.[78]

Second, Weber discerns a mismatch between Wesley's doctrine of salvation and his politics. On this front, Weber suggests that, insofar as Wesley rejected popular sovereignty, he failed to see the political implications of his own soteriology. Thus Weber says,

> In [Wesley's] politics the people have no role, whereas salvation is for all the people. The differences are theological, not practical. In politics divine authorization descends from above, enticing those who are to rule, and excluding the rest. In the way of salvation God elects the entire human race, and offers to equip each person for participation in the work of God. These are fundamental differences, requiring in both cases a transformation of the understanding of the relationship of God to politics, and therefore of the understanding of politics itself.[79]

If Weber is correct in his detection of a twofold inconsistency between Wesley's politics and his theology, then the central claim of this book will be undone. We will have failed to provide an account of Wesley's life and thought on which there is a discernible unity and consistency in his ecclesiastical, political and theological commitments. Thus, we must now examine Wesley's theological commitments. In doing so, we must show that Wesley's doctrine of God was thoroughly consistent with his constitutionalism. Moreover, we must demonstrate that, while Wesley's doctrine of the unlimited atonement by definition offered benefits to all people, it did not of necessity entail popular sovereignty. It is to this task that we now turn.

CHAPTER FOUR

LOVING GOD:
A THEOLOGY OF JOYFUL OBEDIENCE

Christian joy is joy in obedience – joy in loving God and keeping his commandments.

John Wesley, 'The Witness of Our Own Spirit'

The deep thesis in this book is that, to discern the unity and consistency of John Wesley's ecclesiastical, political and theological commitments, we must take seriously the fact that he was an enthusiastic supporter of the confessional state. In other words, Wesley was a product of and contributor to the Anglican hegemony of the long eighteenth century. Thus, in Chapter Two, we suggested that Wesley's relationship to the Church of England must be evaluated not merely with a view towards how well his ministry conformed to church discipline and expectations for clergy conduct, but also with a view towards the political theology of his day – a theology that revolved around the doctrine of the Trinity and the reception of the sacraments.

Having observed that Wesley was firmly committed to the Trinity and sacraments, we acknowledged that, for our case to have merit, we needed to show that Wesley was deeply committed to the English monarchy as well. If it turned out that Wesley opposed English political institutions, then the claim that his ecclesiastical commitments were not merely spiritual and theological but also political in nature would be undermined. Thus, in Chapter Three, we surveyed the history of interpretation of Wesley's politics, noting that the vast majority of recent interpreters have questioned the extent to which Wesley was truly committed to the monarchy. However, in the work of Theodore R. Weber, we discovered a way of reading Wesley's politics that supports our claim that he was deeply committed to the confessional state in which he lived. Yet, if we are finally to make good on our claim, then we must deal with the objections raised by Weber himself concerning the apparent inconsistencies between Wesley's theology and his commitment to the constitutional monarchy. After all, in a confessional state, it is not simply church and state, but it is also theology and politics that go constantly together.

In this chapter, we will provide an overview of the essential ingredients in Wesley's theology. We will maintain that the basic framework of his theology was a form of Arminianism. Within that framework, we will observe that Wesley developed a robust account of the work of the Holy Spirit in bringing people to God, in assuring them of their salvation and in sanctifying and making them holy. Next, we will contend that, in the light of his doctrines of the atonement and the work of the Holy Spirit, Wesley is rightly viewed as a theologian of the economic Trinity. Finally, we will conclude by showing that Wesley's theology and politics are in fact mutually reinforcing. Indeed, we will go so far as to claim that Wesley's Arminianism was tailor-made for the politics of the constitutional monarchy, which is to say, for the confessional state in the long eighteenth century.

BACKGROUND DEVELOPMENTS: ARMINIANISM AND COVENANT THEOLOGY

If we are to see how well Wesley's Arminian theology cohered with the politics of the confessional state in the long eighteenth century, then we must first come to grips with the fact that Arminians, no less than Calvinists, embraced the language and logic of covenant theology. Unfortunately, many people associate covenant theology with Puritanism, not Arminianism. Indeed, some scholars, upon encountering covenantal language in Wesley, have concluded that Wesley himself was influenced by Puritanism.[1] This is understandable enough. Puritanism was thoroughly covenantal. For example, an early Puritan by the name of Paul Bayne wrote, 'The sum of the covenant between God and us is this: God in Christ saith, he will take us for his people, we promise him that we will have him for our God. This therefore doth comprise all our duty to God, that we set him in our hearts.'[2]

However, while covenantalism flourished among the Puritans, it was by no means exclusive to them. On the contrary, the language and logic of covenantalism could be found throughout late seventeenth- and eighteenth-century England. As Gordon Rupp puts it, 'not only Susanna Wesley, but Hoadly and Clarke as well as William Law could talk about the "covenanted terms of salvation".'[3] While we could add numerous others to this list, it is noteworthy that Samuel Walker (1714–1761), the rector of Truro and regular correspondent of John Wesley's, was a strong proponent of covenant theology.[4]

Even more important for our purpose is the extent to which the language and logic of covenant was native to Arminianism. If this has been obscured by the tendency to associate covenantal theology with Puritanism, then it has also been obscured by neglect. Put simply, the origins of Arminian theology are often more assumed than studied carefully. This is especially true of the Remonstrant controversy which, as Nicholas Tyacke puts it, has 'never received the emphasis it deserves from students of English religious history'.[5]

A quick way to get at the Remonstrant controversy is to pay attention to the Synod of Dort. Held in 1618–1619, the Synod of Dort was called in order to settle disputes within the Dutch Calvinist tradition concerning the status of the Remonstrants, who would later come to be known as Arminians, after the name of the early Remonstrant leader, Jacob Arminius. Suffice it to say, the outcome of the Synod of Dort is better known than the content of the confessional statements that resulted on both sides. Thus it is well-known that the Synod rejected Arminianism and affirmed the doctrines of total depravity, unconditional election, limited atonement, irresistible grace and the preservation of the saints (TULIP). Unfortunately, this does not tell us much about the Remonstrant position in the debate.

Failure to pay close attention to the content of the confessional statements that resulted from the Synod of Dort has obscured the fact that we have here to do with an intra-Calvinist dispute. In other words, the Synod of Dort was not called to settle a disagreement between Calvinists and Arminians, as though Arminians did not belong to the Reformed tradition. This is an understandable mistake. After all, the fact that the synod came down so hard against the Arminians gives the impression that there must have been little common ground between the two parties.

In point of fact, the two parties in the dispute shared a common theological language. The Arminians, no less than 'Calvinists', spoke the language of 'covenant' or 'the covenant of grace'. We can see this shared inheritance in the official confessional statements of both groups. Thus the preface to the Canons of Dort (the resulting 'Calvinist' statement) reads: 'Blessed forever be the Lord, who . . . has given witness to the entire world that he does not forget his covenant.'[6] A few years later, the Remonstrant Confession would refer to 'the will of God that is comprehended in the covenant of grace'.[7]

As the resulting confessional statements reveal, the dispute between the parties at Dort was largely over how to understand the covenant of grace. For the 'Calvinist' party, the covenant of grace had to be interpreted within the wider framework of the doctrine of election, according to which God's freedom and sovereignty were expressed in the issuing of eternal divine decrees. Through these eternal divine decrees, some people were eternally predestined for salvation, while everyone else was eternally predestined for damnation.

From the 'Calvinist' standpoint, the doctrine of unconditional double predestination was the best way of demonstrating that the divine will was not subject to any external demands or constraints. However, this also meant that the covenant of grace enacted in the atoning sacrifice of Christ applied only to those who had been eternally predestined for salvation. Moreover, for those predestined to salvation, the covenant of grace was both irresistible and irrevocable. Finally, the doctrine of total depravity meant that none of this was to be taken as evidence that God was unjust. Rather, the fact that God predestined anyone at all to salvation was to be taken as evidence for God's mercy and grace.

The Arminian party was equally concerned to emphasize the freedom and sovereignty of God. Thus they insisted that God was 'free from any internal necessity of his own nature and from any external power of some other force'.[8] However, the Arminian party argued that God's freedom and sovereignty was best expressed within the framework of a doctrine of providence rather than within the framework of the doctrine of election. According to the Arminians, the providence of God was evident in and through the bestowal of grace in both creation and redemption. However, contrary to the 'Calvinist' party, they maintained that God also gave to human individuals the freedom to reject the grace so bestowed in creation and redemption by disobeying God's will. Much of the Arminian argument hinged on the idea that God could not justly punish people for disobeying God's will if God had predetermined before the fall that they would do so. Thus the Arminians concluded,

[The] divine will contained in the covenant of grace . . . comprehends two principle parts: first, what God himself, through Jesus Christ his Son, has decided to do in us or on our behalf, so that we might become participants in the eternal salvation that has been offered through him; second what he wills to be done by us through the mediation of his grace if we really want to attain eternal salvation.[9]

The upshot of the Arminian argument was that God had given humankind a role to play in the covenant of grace manifest initially in creation and again in the redemptive work of Christ. To be sure, the Arminian party insisted that God offered the covenant of grace to every person. Thus, at creation, God entered into covenant with all humankind through Adam. When Adam rejected the covenant, God offered a new covenant of grace to all humankind through the atoning death of Jesus Christ. Yet, just as Adam had been able to reject the covenant on offer in creation, so too could any person reject the covenant of grace on offer in Jesus Christ. Grace, as they would say, is not irresistible. Logically speaking, this meant that one had to do something in order to enjoy the benefits of the covenant of grace. Traditionally, one had to put one's faith in Jesus Christ. As we will see up ahead, much would turn for Wesley on what was meant by faith.

Suffice it to say that the 'Calvinist' party at Dort believed the Arminian position compromised the freedom and sovereignty of God. For their

part, the Arminians insisted that divine freedom meant that God was free
to restrain God's power in order to grant genuine freedom to each individual either to accept or to reject the covenant of grace. Through this
manifestation of divine freedom, the Arminians argued, God revealed
God's self not only as sovereign and free, but as gracious, loving and wise.
Interestingly enough, both the Arminians and the 'Calvinists' could find
support for their views in Calvin.[10]

We see then that Arminianism was about more than the doctrine of
unlimited atonement. If the doctrine of unlimited atonement was a central thread in Arminianism, it was thoroughly embedded in the language
and logic of the covenant of grace. Thus Arminians did not maintain that
the atonement secured salvation for everyone, but that it made salvation
available to everyone. The whole point was to stress that every person had
a role to play in salvation. They had to enter into the covenant of grace
actively and freely. What, according to Wesley, did this entail?

THE COVENANTAL ARMINIAN FRAMEWORK OF WESLEY'S THEOLOGY

If the language and logic of covenant theology was widespread in seventeenth-century England, the Arminian interpretation of the covenant of
grace was not.[11] To be sure, Arminianism was sufficiently present in seventeenth-century England that Puritanism can be viewed partly as a reaction
to 'the incursions of Arminian doctrine into Anglican teaching'. Yet, prior
to 'the rise of Methodism in the eighteenth century', the Arminian interpretation of the covenant of grace was limited to 'the antithetical formula-
tions it evoked' in the *Canons* of the Synod of Dort and the *Westminster
Confession*.[12] Thus it is not an exaggeration to say that one of Wesley's most
significant contributions in English theology was the bringing to full expression of what might most accurately be called *covenantal Arminianism*.

From the start, we can readily acknowledge that the doctrine of universal atonement is the linchpin in Wesley's Arminianism. Remove this
from the equation, and Wesley's whole theology will collapse like a house
of cards. Wesley himself acknowledged as much when he said, 'Nothing
in the Christian system is of greater consequence than the doctrine of
Atonement.'[13]

However, while Wesley was a strong proponent of the universality of
the atonement, he viewed the atonement within the wider framework of
covenant theology. In order to see this clearly, the best place to begin is
not with the atonement itself, but with Wesley's account of creation. There
we can readily see the standard features of covenant theology as refracted
through the Arminian tradition.

When Wesley spoke of creation, he routinely resorted to the language and
logic of covenant theology. Thus he referred to creation as having to do with

'the covenant of works'. The first thing to notice about this aspect of Wesley's doctrine of creation is that, contrary to what we might expect, Wesley did not use 'the covenant of works' to refer to the Mosaic covenant, as though the distinction between the covenant of works and the covenant of grace paralleled a distinction between law and gospel. Rather, Wesley insisted that the covenant of works applied to 'none but Adam before the fall'.[14]

The next thing to notice is that the language of the covenant of works implies a divine will or purpose. For Wesley, the divine will or purpose in creation was expressed most clearly in the moral law. However, this is not nearly as straightforward as it may seem.

At first glance, it is tempting to think that Wesley believed that God gives the moral law in order to maintain goodness and order in the creation. After all, do law and order not go together? Upon closer inspection, however, we discover that, for Wesley, God gives the moral law so that people might know God. Thus Wesley rejects the implied distinction between the moral law and God contained in the old question, does God will the law because it is good or is the law good because God wills it? From Wesley's point of view, 'the whole difficulty' implied in such a question 'arises from considering God's will as distinct from God'. If we do not accept this distinction, he says, the difficulty 'vanishes away'.[15]

For Wesley, the moral law was nothing less than 'an incorruptible picture of the high and holy One that inhabiteth eternity'. The law was 'he whom in his essence no man hath seen or can see, made visible to men and angels'. Moreover, he says that the moral law given at creation is 'the face of God unveiled; God manifested to his creatures as they are able to bear it; manifested to give and not to destroy life; that they may see God and live'. Wesley continues,

> [The moral law] is the heart of God disclosed to man. Yea, in some sense we may apply to this law what the Apostle says of his Son – it is 'the streaming forth' or outbeaming 'of his glory, the express image of his person'.[16]

A little later in this sermon, Wesley equates the law of God with the mind and nature of God, saying, 'The law of God . . . is a copy of the eternal mind, a transcript of the divine nature; yea, it is the fairest offspring of the everlasting Father, the brightest efflux of his eternal wisdom, the visible beauty of the Most High.' He then hastens to add that the moral law, which we now know is a 'picture' or image of God, has three noteworthy properties: 'It is "holy, just, and good".'[17]

Having maintained that the moral law mirrors the 'heart of God', the 'divine nature', and the 'eternal mind', Wesley insists that God created humankind in God's own image and likeness so that the moral law was 'coeval' with their nature. Indeed, says Wesley, God wrote the moral law not upon 'tables of stone, or any corruptible substance', but upon the human heart so that 'it might never be far off, never hard to be understood; but always at hand, and always shining with clear light, even as the sun in the midst of heaven'.[18] Thus Adam was not simply 'capable of God, capable of knowing, loving, and obeying his Creator', but he actually 'did know God, did unfeignedly love and uniformly obey him', so that from this original state and the 'right use of all his faculties, his happiness naturally flowed'.[19] Technically speaking, Wesley referred to this aspect of human nature at creation as the 'moral image' of God.[20]

Although he believed that humans were created in the moral image of God, so that holiness, justice and goodness reigned in their hearts, Wesley also taught that humans were made in the natural image of God. By this he meant that God created individuals with a liberty to choose whether they would go on obeying the moral law within or whether they would reject it. Thus he says,

> Now 'man was made in the image of God'. . . . He was, after the likeness of his Creator, endued with *understanding*, a capacity of apprehending whatever objects were brought before it, and of judging concerning them. He was endued with a *will*, exerting itself in various affections and passions; and lastly, with *liberty*, or freedom of choice, without which all the rest would have been in vain, and he would have been no more capable of serving his Creator than a piece of earth or marble. He would have been as incapable of vice or virtue as any part of the inanimate creation. In these [things] . . . the natural image of God consisted.[21]

Elsewhere, Wesley describes God's gift of freedom to humankind at creation in a way that is consistent with Arminianism, denying that there is any causal relation between eternal divine decrees and the decision of Adam and Eve to reject the moral law. In a sermon on the image of God, Wesley asserts,

> What made his image yet plainer in his human offspring was . . . the liberty he originally enjoyed; the perfect freedom implanted in his nature, and interwoven with all its parts. Man was made with an entire indifference, either to keep or change his first estate: it was left to himself what he would do; his own choice was to determine him in all things. The balance did not incline to one side or the other unless by his own deed. His Creator would not, and no creature besides himself could, weigh down either scale. So that, in this sense, he was the sole lord and sovereign judge of his own actions.[22]

At this stage, Wesley predictably follows the well-worn path in Christian theology of creation, fall and redemption. Thus he turns to the fall from the covenant of works into sin. Of course, for Wesley, it might be more appropriate to speak of a leap into sin, insofar as the language of fall suggests that Adam stumbled into sin accidentally. As we have just seen, Wesley believed that Adam was 'the sole lord and sovereign of his own actions'. Having said this, the most interesting thing to note about Wesley's account of Adam's decision to reject the moral law is the extent to which Wesley is consistent in his equation of the moral law with the presence of God. In other words, in rejecting the law, Adam did not simply reject an impersonal moral code that was enforced by an indifferent judge. Rather, Adam rejected the tie that bound him to God, namely, a heart characterized by love and holiness. Thus Wesley says,

> But it was not long before man rebelled against God, and by breaking this glorious law wellnigh effaced it out of his heart; 'the eyes of his understanding' being *darkened* in the same measure as his soul was 'alienated from the life of God'.[23]

As this passage makes clear, Wesley believed that the consequences of sin were devastating. After the fall, individuals could no longer apprehend the moral of God, which is to say, they could no longer apprehend the image of God or the heart of God. Their souls were now 'alienated from the life of God'.

The inability to apprehend the presence of God within had one additional consequence: people lost their freedom to know, to obey and to love God. In other words, they were now in bondage to sin. Contrary to popular perceptions of Arminianism as implying free will, this consequence of the fall into sin was not lost on Wesley for one moment.[24] It was simply not the case that Wesley believed in anything approximating free will. Indeed, he could describe human bondage to sin as vividly and gruesomely as Augustine or Luther. Thus he writes,

> [Our sins] . . . are chains of iron and fetters of brass. They are wounds wherewith the world, the flesh, and the devil, have gashed and mangled us all over. They are diseases that drink up our blood and spirits, [and] that bring us down to the chambers of the grave.[25]

After noting the devastating consequences of sin, Wesley is quick to observe that God 'did not despise the work of his own hands'. Rather, he says, God once again revealed God's true nature to humankind, 'being reconciled to man through the Son of his love', and thereby '[re-inscribing] the law on the heart of his dark, sinful creature'.[26] In other words, after Adam rejected the covenant of works in creation, God made available a covenant of grace initially through the Mosaic law and ultimately through the life, death and resurrection of Jesus Christ.

In turning to the covenant of grace, Wesley was particularly concerned to stress four things. First, he went out of his way on more than one occasion to insist that the covenant of grace made available in Christ was not to be contrasted with the covenant made available through Moses, but with the covenant of works in creation. For example, in a sermon on Romans 10.5–8, Wesley declares,

> The Apostle does not here oppose the covenant given by Moses to the covenant given by Christ. If we ever imagined this it was for want of observing that the latter as well as the former part of these words were spoken by Moses himself to the people of Israel, and that concerning the covenant which then was. But it is the covenant of *grace* which God through Christ hath established with men in all ages (as well before, and under the Jewish dispensation, as since God was manifest in the flesh), which St. Paul here opposes to the covenant of *works*, made with Adam while in paradise, but commonly supposed to be the only covenant which God had made with man, particularly by those Jews of whom the Apostle writes.[27]

Second, while Wesley frequently stressed the continuity of the covenant of grace 'given by Moses' with the covenant 'given by Christ', he was also clear about what made the latter covenant distinct, namely, its universal scope. The atonement for sin undertaken by Christ on the cross was not for a particular group of individuals, but for all people. In making this move, Wesley was clearly siding with the Arminian over against the 'Calvinist' interpretation of the covenant of grace, especially insofar as the latter interpretation included the doctrine of unconditional double predestination.

As we noted in Chapter One, this is precisely the point over which Wesley and Whitefield fell out. Indeed, the dispute between Wesley and Whitefield resulted in a deep division in the evangelical revival, 'the consequences of which have outlasted the lives of the antagonists'.[28] We can see both positions clearly in the following passage from Wesley's sermon on free grace:

> And, 'The same Lord over all is rich in mercy to all that call upon him.' But you say, 'No: he is such only to those for whom Christ died. And those are not all, but only a few, "whom God hath chosen out of the world"; for he died not for all, but only for those who were "chosen in him before the foundation of the world". Flatly contrary to your interpretation of these Scriptures also is the whole tenor of the New Testament; as are in particular those texts: 'Destroy not him with thy meat for whom Christ died' – a clear proof that Christ died, not only for those that are saved, but also for them that perish; He is 'the Saviour

of the world'; He is 'the Lamb of God, that taketh away the sins of the world'; 'He is the propitiation, not for our sins only, but also for the sins of the whole world;' 'He (the living God) is the Saviour of all men;' 'He gave himself a ransom for all;' 'He tasted death for every man.'[29]

Third, in good Arminian fashion, Wesley denied that the universal or unlimited scope of the atonement necessarily meant that all people would actually be saved. To be sure, it was God's *intention* to save all. Yet, just as Adam was free to reject the covenant of works in creation, so now each individual was free to accept or reject the covenant of grace. The good news now was that one had only to repent of one's sins and to put one's faith in the atoning sacrifice of Christ in order to be saved. In other words, Wesley strongly affirmed the doctrine of justification by faith.

But what, precisely, did Wesley mean by faith? What was the act of faith that justified? The best way to answer this question is to distinguish between faith as intellectual assent to the cognitive contents of Christianity (*assensus*) and faith as personal trust in the atoning sacrifice of Christ for one's sins (*fiducia*). While Wesley did not deny the importance of a careful consideration on the cognitive contents of Christianity, he clearly believed that the faith that justified and therefore saved was of the latter kind, namely, faith as *fiducia* or personal trust. Thus in a very important passage in his sermon 'Salvation by Faith', Wesley writes,

> What faith is it then through which we are saved? It may be answered: first, in general, it is a faith in Christ – Christ, and God through Christ, are the proper object of it. Herein therefore it is sufficiently, absolutely, distinguished from the faith either of ancient or modern heathens. And from the faith of a devil it is fully distinguished by this – it is not barely a speculative, rational thing, a cold, lifeless assent, a train of ideas in the head; but also a disposition of the heart. . . .
> . . . Christian faith is then not only an assent to the whole gospel of Christ, but also a full reliance on the blood of Christ, a trust in the merits of his life, death, and resurrection; a recumbency upon him as our atonement and our life, as *given for us*, and *living in us*. It is a sure confidence which a man hath in God, that through the merits of Christ *his* sins are forgiven, and *he* reconciled to the favour of God; and in consequence hereof a closing with him and cleaving to him as our 'wisdom, righteousness, sanctification, and redemption' or, in one word, our salvation.[30]

By defining faith primarily in terms of personal trust rather than mere intellectual assent, Wesley set the stage for a fourth and final point of emphasis. While it is only the act of putting one's trust in the atoning sacrifice of Christ that justifies or saves, works follow immediately from such an act. As Wesley liked to say, works were not antecedent to justification by faith, but they were an immediate consequence of it.

To help us see this clearly, perhaps an analogy will help. Suppose a person says, 'I have faith in my doctor.' Under normal circumstances, we would take her to mean that she trusts her doctor. However, we would be greatly confused if we discovered later that this same person refused to take the medicine prescribed by her doctor, to follow her doctor's orders to get more exercise, and the like. Indeed, if the person routinely refused to do what her doctor instructed her to do, then we would rightly conclude that she did not really trust her doctor after all.

Wesley's view of the relationship between faith and works mirrors the use of faith in this analogy. At no point does Wesley argue that works are necessary for justification. Rather, he consistently maintains that faith as personal trust is the only thing necessary. Yet, in doing so, Wesley fully expects that works of love and righteousness will immediately follow. In short, Wesley expects that those who have come truly to trust in Christ for their salvation will also be obedient to Christ. Thus, after denying that any man other than Adam was ever under the covenant of works – a covenant that 'required perfect, universal obedience, as the one condition of acceptance, and left no place for pardon, upon the very least transgression' – Wesley says,

> All [God's] sons were and are under the covenant of grace. The manner of their acceptance is this: the free grace of God, through the merits of Christ, gives pardon to them that believe, that believe with such a faith as, working by love, produces all obedience and holiness.

He continues,

> The case is not therefore, as you suppose, that men were *once* more obliged to obey God, or to work the works of his law, than they are *now*. This is a supposition you cannot make good. But we should have been obliged, if we had been under the covenant of works, to have done those works antecedent to our acceptance. Whereas now all good works, though as necessary as ever, are not antecedent to our acceptance, but consequent upon it. Therefore the nature of the covenant of grace gives you no ground, no encouragement at all, to set aside any instance or degree of obedience, and part or measure of holiness.[31]

We can now see the basic covenantal Arminian framework of Wesley's theology, including the covenant of works at creation, the gift of liberty or freedom to accept or reject that covenant, the fall into sin and the resulting situation of total depravity, the covenant of grace made available to all through Christ, the doctrine of justification by faith and the insistence that obedience or works was the evidence of true faith. We can also see why Wesley's Arminianism did not lead to a broad egalitarianism without qualifications and conditions. On Wesley's analysis, salvation was for every person, but it was conditioned on repentance, trusting faith and obedience. Without obedience, there was no real faith, and without faith the universal scope of salvation went unrealized.

At this stage, it is tempting to make comparisons with Wesley's politics. We can already hear the resonances between covenantal Arminianism and the politics of constitutional monarchianism. However, were we to stop now, we would not have the full picture of Wesley's theology. Suffice it to say that, within the framework of his covenantal Arminianism, Wesley found himself constantly dealing with three big questions. First, given the devastating consequences of sin both for our ability to apprehend God and our freedom to respond favourably to God, how is it possible for one to apprehend and respond to the covenant of grace made available in Christ? Second, supposing that a person can apprehend and respond to the covenant of grace made available in Christ, how can she know that she has responded adequately? In other words, how can she be assured that she has truly put her faith in Christ and that she is therefore saved? Third, once a person has truly put her faith in Christ and begun to express that faith through obedience, what is left to do? What is the ultimate goal for the Christian life?

In many ways, these three questions occupied Wesley off and on throughout his life. For example, Wesley struggled with the second question throughout the early part of his ministry. Thus he was constantly trying to figure out whether he really had faith. Over time, Wesley answered all three questions in ways that often proved controversial. For better or worse, he filled in the crucial gaps in his covenantal Arminian theology by developing a robust account of the work of the Holy Spirit. It is to this very important aspect of Wesley's theology that we must now turn.

THE HOLY SPIRIT AND THE CHRISTIAN LIFE

It is sometimes said that, as a theologian, John Wesley specialized in the doctrine of the Christian life. It would be more accurate to say that he specialized in theology *for* the Christian life. Thus Wesley's most interesting contributions to theology were all motivated by a desire to help people discover the riches of the Christian life for themselves. After all, people had real questions and concerns. How could they move from sin to salvation when sin blinded them from discerning the covenant of grace in the first place? How could they be assured that they were justified in the eyes of God? How could they come truly to flourish in love for God and neighbour? These were all practical questions that related directly to the Christian life. In answering them, Wesley tried to help people navigate their way through some perplexing theological terrain in the journey of salvation.

The first question on our list was triggered by the doctrine of total depravity. On Wesley's own analysis, total depravity meant that people were incapable of discerning, much less accepting and entering into, the covenant of grace. Complicating matters further was Wesley's definition of faith as personal trust in God for salvation rather than mere intellectual assent. Wesley was clearly not prepared to say that entry into the covenant of grace was simply a matter of assent to propositions, even if those propositions had to do with the person and work of Jesus Christ. Salvation was not simply a matter of adding on a few new beliefs. Rather, entering into the covenant of grace was more like being born all over again. Thus, Wesley says,

> Before a child is born into the world he has eyes, but sees not; he has ears, but does not hear. He has a very imperfect use of any other sense. He has no knowledge of any of the things of the world, nor any natural understanding. To that manner of existence which he then has we do not even give the name of life. It is then only when a man is born that we say, he begins to live. For as soon as he is born he begins to see the light and the various objects with which he is encompassed. His ears are then opened, and he hears the sounds which successively strike upon them. At the same time all the other organs of sense begin to be exercised upon their proper objects. He likewise breathes and lives in a manner wholly different from what he did before. How exactly does the parallel hold in all these instances! While a man is in a mere natural state, before he is born of God, he has, in a spiritual sense, eyes and sees not; a thick impenetrable veil lies upon them. He has ears, but hears not; he is utterly deaf to what he is most of all concerned to hear. His other spiritual senses are all locked up; he is in the same condition as if he had them not. Hence he has no knowledge of God, no intercourse with him; he is not at all acquainted with him. He has no true knowledge of the things of God, either of spiritual or eternal things. Therefore, though he is a living man, he is a dead Christian.[32]

Here Wesley portrays the consequences of the fall into sin in terms of a complete imprisonment of the spiritual senses. Thus he says that one's spiritual senses are so 'locked up' that they are 'in the same condition as if [one] had them not'. If this was the case, then how could one possibly come to apprehend the covenant of grace and begin to live therein?

To address this question, Wesley instinctively turned to the person and work of the Holy Spirit. Being born again, he informs his readers, requires nothing less than 'the mighty working of the Spirit of God' within the human heart. According to Wesley, the Holy Spirit restores the spiritual

WESLEY: A GUIDE FOR THE PERPLEXED

senses, enabling one to see 'the light of the glory of God . . . in the face of Jesus Christ' and to hear 'the inward voice of God, saying, "Be of good cheer, thy sins are forgiven thee": "Go and sin no more."' When this happens, says Wesley, individuals become conscious of 'a peace which passeth all understanding', and they feel 'a joy in God', as well as 'the love of God shed abroad' in their hearts 'by the Holy Ghost which is given unto [them]'. Moreover, through the Spirit's rehabilitation of the spiritual senses, they begin 'to discern spiritual "good and evil"' and daily to increase 'in the knowledge of God, of Jesus Christ whom he hath sent, and of all the things pertaining to his inward kingdom'. Only then can they 'properly be said *to live*: God having quickened [them] by his Spirit, [they are] alive to God through Jesus Christ'. Finally, Wesley insisted that the Spirit does not depart after awakening the spiritual senses. Thus he developed and deployed a doctrine of spiritual respiration to describe a person's life after the new birth as follows:

> God is continually breathing, as it were, upon his soul, and his soul is breathing unto God. Grace is descending into his heart, and prayer and praise ascending to heaven. And by this intercourse between God and man, this fellowship with the Father and the Son, as by a kind of spiritual respiration, the life of God in the soul is sustained: and the child of God grows up, till he comes to 'the full measure of the stature of Christ'.[33]

Before we move on to the second question that arose within Wesley's covenantal Arminian framework, two observations are in order. On the one hand, it is important to note that Wesley clearly believed that people were incapable of discerning, much less entering into the covenant of grace on their own accord. Because of the devastating effects of the fall, the Holy Spirit must restore the spiritual senses, enabling them to discern the covenant of grace and assisting them to respond favourably to it. While the technical term for this was prevenient grace, it should be duly noted that, at the level of the restoration of the spiritual senses, it was also irresistible grace. To be sure, they could reject the covenant of grace that they were able to discern with their newly restored faculties, but they could not reject the initial restoration of the faculties by the Holy Spirit.

On the other hand, we should note that Wesley did not simply invent the appeal to the work of the Holy Spirit within the human heart. Rather, he was by his own admission retrieving the riches of the Anglican theological tradition within his covenantal Arminian framework. Thus when he introduces the appeal to the person and work of the Holy Spirit, he tells his readers that he is using 'the language of our Church'.[34] This in itself was no mean feat, as the doctrine of the Holy Spirit had been idling for more than a century in many quarters within Anglicanism.[35]

The second question which naturally emerged within Wesley's covenantal Arminianism had to do with the doctrine of assurance. As noted
in Chapter One, Wesley himself wrestled with the problem of assurance
at a very personal level. In doing so, he was hardly alone. Seventeenth-
and eighteenth-century English Protestant theologians on all sides were
wrestling with the question, how could people be assured that they were
saved?[36] More precisely, on the 'Calvinist' side, theologians wrestled
with the question, how could people be sure they were among the elect?
On the Arminian side, the question took the form, how could people
be sure they had met the condition for salvation, namely, faith in Jesus
Christ?

The prevalence of this question in seventeenth- and eighteenth-century
England was due in large part to the Calvinist doctrine of divine inscrutability. For many people, the inscrutability of the divine will led to an
anguishing uncertainty concerning whether they were among the elect.
In some cases, this uncertainty even led to suicide. Thus Arminianism
became influential in seventeenth-century England in part because
it offered an alternative solution for the problem of assurance. Many
Arminians insisted that, if individuals met the condition of the covenant
of grace, then they could be sure of their salvation. That condition, as we
have already seen, was putting their faith in the atoning blood of Jesus
Christ. However, seventeenth-century Anglican theologians influenced by
Arminianism tended to define faith in terms of intellectual assent. This
was especially fitting, they argued, because the covenant of grace was
available to all. If all people were endowed with reason, then all people
were capable of giving intellectual assent to the clear and intelligible propositions contained in scripture.[37]

As we have seen, Wesley was not content with faith as assent. While
faith involved assent, it also had a deeper, more demanding dimension –
personal trust in God. Thus, despite his insistence on the importance of
belief in the Trinity, Wesley was clear that mere belief was not enough. For
example, in a sermon called 'The Way to the Kingdom', he says,

> For neither does religion consist in *orthodoxy* or *right opinions*; which,
> although they are not properly outward things, are not in the heart, but
> the understanding. A man may be orthodox in every point; he many
> not only espouse right opinions, but zealously defend them against all
> opposers; he may think justly concerning the incarnation of our Lord,
> concerning the ever blessed Trinity, and every other doctrine contained
> in the oracles of God. He may assent to all the three creeds – that called
> the Apostles', the Nicene, and the Athanasian – and yet 'tis possible he
> may have no religion at all, no more than a Jew, Turk, or pagan. He may
> be almost as orthodox as the devil . . . and may all the while be as great
> a stranger as he to the religion of the heart.[38]

If assent to orthodox Christian doctrine was not the criterion of assurance, then what was? What evidence could a person assess to determine whether they had moved from a religion of the head to religion of the heart? How could they be sure that they trusted God for their salvation in the relevant way or to the right degree?

We noted a moment ago that Wesley believed that saving faith depended on the inner working of the Holy Spirit awakening the spiritual senses within. Consequently, we might expect that Wesley would have solved the problem of assurance simply by appealing to the fruits of the Spirit. If the Spirit was at work within people to the degree that Wesley described in his doctrine of spiritual respiration, then surely there would be evidence of such a thing in their lives. Wesley himself was well aware of this possibility, saying,

> The Word of God says everyone who has the fruit of the Spirit is a child of God. Experience, or inward consciousness, tells me that I have the fruit of the Spirit. And hence I rationally conclude: therefore I am a child of God.[39]

However, despite his insistence on the importance of the fruits of the Spirit, Wesley refused to make this the criterion of assurance. On the one hand, he insisted that there could be no 'real testimony of the Spirit without the fruit of the Spirit'.[40] On the other hand, he judged appeals to the fruit of the Spirit as evidence for salvation to be one more rational argument, the ' "witness of our spirit", our reason or understanding'.[41]

If Wesley could not make the fruits of the Spirit the criterion of assurance, then it was likely because he had been down that road himself. He knew personally that this could lead to an obsession with taking one's own spiritual temperature. More importantly, having done this for years, he knew that the fruits of the Spirit could wax and wane. Thus he says, 'Neither joy nor peace are always at one stay; no, nor love; as neither is the testimony itself always equally strong and clear.'[42]

For Wesley, the solution to the problem of assurance lay in recognizing that 'the testimony of the Spirit must, in the very nature of things, be antecedent to "the testimony of our own spirit".' Wesley continues,

> We must be holy in heart and life before we can be conscious that we are so. But we must love God before we can be holy at all, this being the root of all holiness. Now we cannot love God till we know he loves us. . . . And we cannot know his love to us till his Spirit witnesses it to our spirit.[43]

Here we meet with the reason that Wesley was sometimes charged with enthusiasm. He solved the problem of assurance by appeal to the direct inner witness or testimony of the Spirit. In other words, he appealed to spiritual intuitionism, according to which individuals could be conscious of the presence and work of the Holy Spirit assuring them that they were children of God. Thus Wesley says, 'The sum of all is this: the testimony of the Spirit is an inward impression on the souls of believers, whereby the Spirit of God directly testifies to their spirit that they are children of God.'[44]

If Wesley separated the testimony of the Spirit and the fruits of the Spirit in an attempt to deal with the problem of assurance, he clearly believed that the two had quickly to be reunited. What could be momentarily separated in thought could not be separated in the Christian life. Thus on the one hand he cautioned,

> Let none rest in any supposed fruit of the Spirit without the witness. There may be foretastes of joy, of peace, of love – and those not delusive, but really from God – long before we have the witness in ourselves, before the Spirit of God witnesses with our spirits that we have 'redemption in the blood of Jesus, even the forgiveness of sins'.[45]

On the other hand he warned,

> Let none ever presume to rest in any supposed testimony of the Spirit which is separate from the fruit of it. If the Spirit of God does really testify that we are children of God, the immediate consequence will be the fruit of the Spirit, even 'love, joy, peace, long-suffering, gentleness, goodness, fidelity, meekness, temperance'.[46]

In wrestling with problems related to faith and assurance, Wesley returned again and again to the person and work of the Holy Spirit. Indeed, it would not be too much to say that the Holy Spirit was the touchstone of his doctrine of the Christian life. And while there is ample precedent for virtually every aspect of his pneumatology in English Protestant theology in both its Anglican and Puritan forms, the pervasiveness of pneumatology in Wesley's theology was mostly unique to him. Few theologians in seventeenth- or eighteenth-century England had as robust a doctrine of the Holy Spirit as John Wesley.[47]

Having made faith and assurance dependent on the work of the Holy Spirit within human hearts, and having insisted that these were accompanied by the fruits of the Spirit in human lives, a third set of closely related questions naturally arose. Given Wesley's definition of faith as personal trust, to what extent should persons of faith be expected to keep the commandments of God? To what degree should the fruits of the Spirit be evident in the lives of the children of God? To what extent did participation in the covenant of grace result in the transformation of human lives and living? If the Spirit was able to restore the spiritual senses and to assist one in discerning and embracing the covenant of grace, then what else was the Spirit capable of? In short, was there a limit to what the Spirit could do in one's life? In attempting to answer these questions, Wesley formulated what would quickly become the most controversial aspect of his theology, namely, the doctrine of entire sanctification.

One way to get at the heart of Wesley's understanding of entire sanctification or Christian perfection is simply to extend the medical analogy we have been using to help explain Wesley's view of true faith. Whereas doctors prescribe medicine for their patients' physical healing and well-being, Wesley believed that 'Christ had ordained certain outward means for conveying his grace into the souls of men.'[48] These 'means of grace', he says, are 'outward signs, words, or actions ordained of God, and appointed for this end – to be the *ordinary* channels whereby he might convey to men preventing, justifying, or sanctifying grace'.[49]

As in so many other areas of his theology, it is interesting to note that Wesley went out of his way to point out that, in referring to the means of grace, he was using a term that was particularly native to 'our own church'. Moreover, he went on to provide the standard Anglican list of the means of grace, saying,

> The chief of these means are prayer, whether in secret or with the great congregation; searching the Scriptures (which implies reading, hearing, and meditating thereon) and receiving the Lord's Supper, eating bread and drinking wine in remembrance of him; and these we believe to be ordained of God as the ordinary channels of conveying his grace to the souls of men.[50]

The most important thing to note about the means of grace, however, is Wesley's insistence that the 'end' for which they were given is what ultimately matters. Indeed, Wesley was clearly worried about the possibility that people might mistake the means of grace for the essence of religion. Thus he writes,

> But we allow that the whole value of the means depends on their actual subservience to the end of religion; that consequently all these means, when separate from the end, are less than nothing, and vanity; that if they do not actually conduce to the knowledge and love of God they are not acceptable in his sight; yea, rather, they are an abomination before him; a stink in his nostrils; he is weary to bear them – above all if they are used as a kind of 'commutation' for the religion they were designed to subserve.[51]

Despite this worry, there is abundant evidence that Wesley highly valued the means of grace. For example, as we saw in Chapter One, Wesley left the Fetter Lane Society precisely because they discontinued the use of the means of grace. And while Wesley's departure from Fetter Lane suggests that he valued the means of grace for justification, he clearly emphasized their role in entire sanctification and Christian perfection as well.[52]

As Wesley's warning about the means of grace demonstrates, he believed that the essence and goal of religion was the knowledge and love of God, not outward obedience per se. Indeed, Wesley repeatedly said that what really mattered in religion was love for God and love for neighbour. Moreover, as we have seen, he was convinced that obedience followed a change of heart. It was the consequence of a right ordering of one's affections. Yet there is a real sense in which obedience and love are in a dialectical relationship in Wesley's theology. This is especially true in his view of the means of grace. Thus, on the one hand, he insists that participation in the means of grace was most beneficial when it was done out of love. On the other hand, however, he believes that the Spirit works through the means of grace to bring about an ever-deepening love for God and neighbour in the human heart.

If Wesley believed that the essence and goal of religion was the filling full of the human heart with love for God and neighbour, and if he believed that the Spirit worked in and through the means of grace toward that end, then he also insisted that sanctification did not happen automatically. In other words, taking the sacraments or participating in the means of grace did not automatically result in the complete transformation of the heart. While Christians were responsible for obeying the commands of Christ to participate in the means of grace, it was the Spirit who brought about the changing of their hearts. Thus we do not have to do here with sanctification by works. On the contrary, Wesley clearly taught that sanctification was as much a matter of grace as justification. For this reason, he stressed the relative unpredictability of sanctification, saying,

> There is likewise great variety in the manner and time of God's bestowing his *sanctifying grace*, whereby he enables his children to give him their whole heart, which we can in no wise account for. We know not why he bestows this on some even before they ask for it (some unquestionable instances of which we have seen); on some after they have sought it but a few days; and yet permits other believers to wait for it perhaps twenty, thirty, or forty years; nay, and others till a few hours or even minutes before their spirits return to him.[53]

Allowing for the unpredictability of sanctifying grace, what exactly did Wesley have in mind when he spoke of entire sanctification or Christian perfection? We have been hinting at this all along. For example, his understanding of entire sanctification shows up in his comment about the knowledge and love of God being 'the end of religion', and in his remark about the varying lengths of time it takes for people to give God their whole hearts. To be sure, Wesley sometimes spoke of entire sanctification in terms of freedom from sinful thoughts. Yet, he regarded entire sanctification or Christian perfection as having above all to do with the filling of the human heart with love for God and neighbour and the governing of all subsequent thoughts, words and deeds, by that love. Thus, in one of his most straightforward comments on the subject, he says, 'By perfection, I mean the humble, gentle, patient love of God and man ruling all the tempers, words, and actions, the whole heart and the whole life.'[54]

Sadly, Wesley's doctrine of entire sanctification was a matter of controversy and debate for most of the latter half of his life. Moreover, it has been a matter of intense and at times acrimonious debate among his ecclesiastical descendents. Indeed, deep divisions over the doctrine of sanctification have occurred across the centuries within various Wesleyan and Methodist communions. These divisions have often been so painful that many Wesleyan and Methodist communions have all but ceased talking about the doctrine that Wesley claimed was the reason that God raised up the people called Methodists in the first place. Thus, in many Wesleyan and Methodist circles, talking about sanctification at clergy conferences and in local churches is like talking about politics at a dinner party. It is the sort of thing people avoid lest they start a fight on an otherwise pleasant occasion.

What is particularly tragic here is that, in most of the debates over sanctification, the antagonists have missed the forest for the trees. In not a few instances, they have missed the forest for the bark on a particular tree. For example, a most controversial matter has to do with whether entire sanctification occurs in a moment or through a process. This particular debate stems largely from two sentences in a letter that John wrote to his brother Charles. The sentences read: 'As to the manner, I believe this perfection is always wrought in the soul by faith, by a simple act of faith; consequently in an instant. But I believe a gradual work both preceding and following that instant.'[55]

Suffice it to say that these sentences are too often read as though they were in a manual for defusing a bomb. In other words, they are read as though every word or phrase is a wire that must either be cut or left alone. One word is green, the next yellow. This phrase represents a purple wire, that one a blue wire. Cut the wrong wire, and the consequences are devastating. The whole of Wesley's doctrine of sanctification explodes into a million pieces.

My own inclination is that Wesley did not intend this letter to be taken as literally as it has. Moreover, I suspect that he would be shocked to learn that so much fuss has been made over two sentences, and I am certain that he would be disappointed that the debates over these two sentences have caused many to steer clear of the doctrine altogether.

How, then, should we read these two sentences? Put simply, when reading these two sentences, one should recall that, for Wesley, sanctification was ultimately the work of the Holy Spirit. It was therefore a gift to be received. As such, I am confident that Wesley would have been horrified by any dogged insistence that the Holy Spirit must give the gift in a particular way – say, through a process or in a moment. Whatever else Wesley believed about the Holy Spirit, he clearly took seriously the Scriptural attributions of power *and* freedom of movement to the Spirit. To be sure, he insisted on the Spirit's power entirely to sanctify a person in a moment, but he also insisted that the Spirit was free to sanctify when, where and how she pleased.

Finally, as to the logic-chopping insistence that there must nevertheless be a moment at which a person is entirely sanctified, we might note that this is like saying that there is some moment at which a person ceases to be an adolescent and becomes a grown man or woman. There are rites of passage and other indicators, to be sure, but where is the line exactly that marks off adolescence from adulthood? Better yet, it is like saying there is some moment at which two persons love one another maximally. To the degree that sanctification has to do with love, logic breaks down entirely the moment we notice that love is not the sort of thing that has a ceiling or some other limit. It is not like, say, a sauce pan than can hold so much and no more. Thus people often say that they know the moment at which they fell in love. Yet, when probed, they will sometimes say that there were subsequent moments at which they fell in love with one another in ways they did not previously know existed. Suffice it to say that, if there are often unsounded depths in the love that exists between individuals, then surely this is infinitely multiplied when we are dealing with the love that exists between human individuals and God.

Now that we have seen the significance of the doctrines of the atonement and the work of the Holy Spirit in Wesley's theology, the time has come to stand back and make two summary observations. First, we need to see the Trinitarian nature of Wesley's covenantal Arminian theology. Second, we need to notice the extent to which Wesley's covenantal Arminianism cohered with and supported the politics of the confessional state.

GOD BEFORE US: THE TRINITARIAN NATURE OF WESLEY'S THEOLOGY

At first glance, covenantal Arminianism can appear to be rationalistic and calculating, as though salvation was a matter of the going exchange rate. By now, we should be able to see that, in Wesley's hands, covenantal Arminianism was primarily, if not entirely, a matter of free grace, not free will. It was from beginning to end a matter of divine gratuity and generosity. Indeed, the whole of Wesley's theology can be captured in the unsettling little phrase, 'while we were yet sinners'.[56] To the extent this is the case, Wesley is best viewed as a Trinitarian theologian.

The suggestion that Wesley is best viewed as a Trinitarian theologian will no doubt come as a surprise to many readers. Surely Trinintarian theology is much too heady for a revival preacher like John Wesley. Surely we are not suggesting that Wesley ever wrote anything about the Trinity on a par with Augustine's *De Trinitate*.

The truth is that Wesley produced no single work of significance on the Trinity. Moreover, he showed virtually no interest in the heady debates about the Trinity that took place in late seventeenth and early eighteenth-century England. Unlike William Sherlock, John Wallis and Edward Stillingfleet, he never attempted to solve the great problem of the principle of individuation.[57] In other words, he never suggested a principle on which the three divine persons could be individuated without dividing the unity of the being of God and without making their individual identities a mere chimera. On the contrary, Wesley clearly preferred to avoid attempts to explain the manner of the divine relations. Thus he could say, 'I would insist only on the direct words unexplained', namely that 'There are three that bear record in heaven, the Father, the Word, and the Holy Ghost: and these three are one.'[58] Most famously, he once exclaimed to a Miss March that

> the mystery does not lie in the fact 'These Three are One', but in the manner [and] the accounting how they are one. But with this I have nothing to do. I believe the fact. As to the manner (wherein the whole mystery lies) I believe nothing about it.[59]

Based on these and other similar statements, it would seem that Wesley did not give one whit about the Trinity. On those few occasions when he did manage to comment on the Trinity, Wesley appears to support a very traditional Western hierarchical view in which the Son proceeds from the Father and the Spirit from the Father and the Son. In other words, Wesley very clearly supported the *filioque* clause inserted in the third article of the Nicene Creed by the Third Council of Toledo in 589.

In what sense, then, can we justify the claim that Wesley was a Trinitarian theologian? Suffice it to say that, while Wesley was not particularly interested in the manner of the relations between the three persons of the Godhead (the so-called immanent Trinity), he was clearly interested in the relations between the three persons of the Godhead and human persons (the so-called economic Trinity). For example, while Wesley attributed the work of assurance to the witness of the Holy Spirit, he did so in a way that related persons directly to the Father and the Son as well. Thus he says,

> But I know not how anyone can be a Christian believer till 'he hath' (as St John speaks) 'the witness in himself'; till 'the Spirit of God witnesses with his spirit that he is a child of God' – that is, in effect, till God the Holy Ghost witnesses that God the Father has accepted him through

the merits of God the Son – and having this witness he honours the Son and the blessed Spirit 'even as he honours the Father'.[60]

Above all, however, Wesley was a theologian of the economic Trinity insofar as his theology revolved around the sheer generosity and gratuity of the Father, Son and Holy Spirit in rescuing, redeeming and rehabilitating fallen humanity. To see this clearly, we need only recall that economic Trinitarian theology is, by definition, concerned with the ways in which God is *for* us.[61] In this sense, Wesley's theology is Trinitarian to the core. Indeed, Wesley's God is not just *for* us, he is ever and always *before* us. Thus Wesley frequently stressed that, while we were sinners, the Father sent the Son as an atoning sacrifice for the sins of the world. Moreover, he maintained that, while we were sinners, the Father and the Son (Wesley would have put it this way) sent the Holy Spirit to awaken the spiritual senses, to enable people to see the love of God in Christ poured out for them on the cross, to assist them in the work of repentance and of putting their trust in Christ, to help them to discern the loving nature of their heavenly Father, to give them the means of grace and through those means to make their hearts and minds conform in obedience and love to the mind of Christ himself. In all of these ways, Wesley's God is a God who is ever going *before* us.

Having said all of this, no economic Trinitarian theology is complete without an equal emphasis on human response to the overtures of God. Here, too, Wesley proved himself thoroughly Trinitarian. Thus he expended an enormous amount of creative energy mapping the soul's journey back to God. As we have seen, he provided thick descriptions of what it is like to be awakened, born again, renewed in the image and likeness of God, sanctified, to have communion with the Father, Son and Holy Spirit, and to have one's heart filled to overflowing with love for God and neighbour. Moreover, while Wesley developed and deployed countless general descriptions of the various stages of the journey of salvation, he was also fond of observing and recording the experiences of individuals along these lines. For example, he observed that a man named Charles Perronet had been led by the Spirit to 'Jesus the Mediator', after which he enjoyed 'communion with the Father, next with the Spirit, and then with the whole Trinity'.[62] This is merely one of hundreds, if not thousands, of cases that Wesley observed and commented on across the years.[63]

Taken together, the sheer gratuity and generosity of God on the one hand, and the mystery and magnitude of salvation on the other was, in Wesley's mind, enough to fill the human heart with gratitude and joy. In turn, the gratitude and joy that filled the human heart expressed itself in and through obedience. Indeed, Wesley was convinced that, once people discerned that God was in every way *for* them – and this despite the fact that they had done nothing to merit divine favour – they would see that the divine commands were intended for their benefit; that joy and peace and love and true liberty came through obedience. As he said,

> Christian joy is joy in obedience – joy in loving God and keeping his commandments. And yet not in keeping them as if we were thereby to fulfil the terms of the *covenant of works*; as if by any works or righteousness of ours we were to *procure* pardon and acceptance with God. Not so: we are already pardoned and accepted through the mercy of God in Christ Jesus – not as if we were by our own obedience to *procure* life, life from the death of sin. This also we have already through the grace of God. . . . And now we are 'alive to God, through Jesus Christ our Lord'. But we rejoice in walking according to the *covenant of grace*, in holy love and happy obedience.[64]

COVENANTAL ARMINIANISM AND THE POLITICS OF THE CONFESSIONAL STATE

We are now in a position to respond to Weber's assertion that there is a twofold incoherence between John Wesley's theology and his politics. In doing so, we will see that there was actually a deep logical coherence between Wesley's covenantal Arminian theology and his constitutionalism. By extension, we will see that Wesley's covenantal Arminianism was tailor-made for the politics of the confessional state in which he lived.

We recall from the end of the previous chapter that, according to Weber, Wesley's God was 'a hierarchical first person of the Trinity – above us, judging, dispensing, disposing'.[65] As such, it was a mismatch for Wesley's constitutionalism. Thus Weber says,

> A hierarchical theology of politics that ordains the peak of power in society with supreme authority does not cohere with a political system designed to control dominant power and diversify authority, that is to say, a constitutional system.[66]

The problem with this criticism is that Wesley's primary concern was with the doctrine of the economic Trinity. To be sure, Wesley thought of the economic Trinity in hierarchal ways. Thus he could speak of the Father sending the Son and of the Father and the Son sending the Spirit. Yet, within the economy of salvation, he most certainly did not portray God the Father primarily as 'above us, judging, dispensing, disposing'. Rather, it is the Father who, out of sheer generosity and love, sends the Son and the Spirit to rescue, redeem and restore fallen humanity. Moreover, while the Father's sending of the Son and the Spirit suggests authority over them (hierarchy), there is a ready analogue here for the constitution's role in limiting the authority of the King, namely, the covenant of grace enacted by the Son and witnessed to by the Spirit. Thus, while a hierarchal conception of God remains, it is not a conception in which God is free to exercise absolute power in God's relations to individuals. Rather, it is hierarchical conception in which God freely agrees to limit God's power in accordance with a covenant, provided that individuals embrace that covenant by putting their trust in and obeying the enactor of that covenant.

We can see, then, that there is a deep logical compatibility between Wesley's economic Trinitarianism and his constitutional monarchianism. Just as the constitution restricts the absolute power of the King, so the atoning blood of Christ constrains the absolute power of God. Moreover, because the constitution precedes the birth of English subjects, the rights and liberties that it grants can in no way be thought of as deserved. Similarly, because the covenant of grace precedes the birth of all people, its benefits are a matter of sheer divine generosity. In both cases, the appropriate response is gratitude and joyful obedience.

The second incoherence that Weber perceives has to do with the doctrine of the unlimited atonement. In Wesley's politics, says Weber, 'the people have no role', whereas in his theology 'salvation is for all the people'.[67] Here Weber is mixing apples and oranges. The parallel that needs to be drawn here is between the English constitution and the atoning work of Christ. If we keep our eyes fixed on this parallel, then we can see that there is no inconsistency here. Both the constitution and the atoning work of Christ are, in a manner of speaking, universal. The constitution does not simply extend rights and liberties to the nobility. Rather the constitution extends rights and liberties to all natural-born English subjects who are obedient to it. Similarly, the atonement is unlimited, extending the offer of salvation to all who respond in trusting faith and in obedience. In each case, the 'role' of the people is the same. They are to respond in obedience. Beyond this, the atonement does not in and of itself confer any additional roles to the people either in the church or in society. Thus, insofar as Wesley's views of the constitution and of the covenant of grace were mutually reinforcing, there was nothing in the doctrine of the unlimited atonement that made popular sovereignty a necessity.

In summary, Wesley's covenantal Arminianism was tailor-made for his constitutionalism and for the confessional state in the long eighteenth century. The covenant of grace and the constitution were both matters of divine gratuity and generosity. Their privileges were neither earned nor deserved. In each case, the appropriate response was joyful obedience. It was good to be a child of God, and it was good to be a subject of the King. All that is left to see is that, for Wesley, the relationships between church and state, God and King, and theology and politics were not limited to their logical similarities.

CONCLUSION

Who was John Wesley? What did he believe? To what and to whom was he committed? These are just some of the questions that have surfaced throughout this book. As we have seen, how we answer these questions depends a great deal on our background assumptions about the age in which Wesley lived.

All too often, Wesley is approached as though he were either timeless or as though he were our contemporary. Either way, the results are the same. Wesley winds up fragmented, inconsistent and at times downright incomprehensible. For example, if we read Wesley from the standpoint of a modern liberal politics in which there is a clean separation between church and state, then we cannot imagine any grounds on which Wesley's insistence that he was a Church of England man makes sense. It simply does not occur to us that, in the long eighteenth century, the criteria for determining loyalty to the established church might have turned on more than sensibilities concerning clergy conduct.

In the preceding chapters, I have maintained that Wesley makes a great deal more sense when we interpret him against the backdrop of a confessional state, which is to say, against the backdrop of an age in which church and state, God and King, and theology and politics went constantly together. Against this backdrop, I have argued that Wesley's ecclesiastical, political and theological commitments are interrelated, mutually reinforcing and generally of a piece with each other. Moreover, I have suggested that this was entirely in keeping with the air that he breathed. On this reading of Wesley, the interpretive challenge is that every ecclesiastical statement must be monitored for its political and theological significance, every political statement for its theological and ecclesiastical implications and every theological statement for its ecclesiastical and political significance. Such was the world in which Wesley lived and moved and had his being.

Looking back, it is possible to notice logical similarities in Wesley's thinking about the established church, the constitution, and the covenant of grace. First and foremost, he clearly regarded all three in terms of the logic of prevenience. Thus, the Church of England was there *before* the revival and the Methodist societies, the constitution was there *before* every natural born English subject, and the covenant of grace was there *before* all people everywhere. Second, he clearly believed that all three offered gifts and privileges and that these offerings were, on the logic of prevenience, a matter of grace. Thus the Church offered doctrine, the liturgy and the sacraments, the constitution offered rights and liberties, and the covenant of grace offered salvation. Third, he believed that in every case the appropriate response to the gratuitous offering of gifts was loyalty and joyful obedience.

The question that now remains is whether there were more than logical similarities in Wesley's view of the church, the constitution, and the covenant of grace. In other words, is there a deeper vision in which all three were intimately related? I believe there is.

One way to think about Wesley is to see in back of his covenantal Arminianism an especially robust doctrine of divine providence. Indeed, throughout his life, his words and actions suggest as much. Wesley could detect the guiding voice or hand of God in almost anything. Having said this, he clearly regarded some things as especially providential. And while the covenant of grace was at the top of his list, it can be argued that the Church of England, the King and the constitution followed closely behind.

There are at least three major benefits of viewing Wesley this way. First, by assigning the established church, the king and the constitution a prominent place in Wesley's list of the workings of divine providence, we can discern in Wesley a unity of thought and action across ecclesiastical, political and theological lines. In turn, we can make sense out of what otherwise seem like very bizarre statements. For example, we can make sense out of Wesley's claim that if a person 'does not love the King, he cannot love God'.[1] Similarly, we can take Wesley at his word when he says,

It is my religion which obliges me 'to put men in mind to be subject to principalities and powers'. Loyalty is with me an essential branch of religion, and which I am sorry any Methodist should forget. There is the closest connexion therefore, between my religious and political conduct; the selfsame authority enjoining me to 'fear God', and to 'honour the King'.[2]

A second benefit of viewing Wesley this way is that it coheres well with the age in which he lived. Indeed, it is hard to imagine statements more in keeping with the political theology of a confessional state than the two just quoted. Moving in the other direction, it is hard to imagine a successful confessional state that does not have within its political theology a robust doctrine of divine providence. Thus, to the extent that Wesley had such a doctrine, he was utterly at home in the long eighteenth century.

A third major benefit of detecting in Wesley a robust doctrine of providence is that it enables us better to understand and to appreciate the dilemma that he faced with Methodism. As we saw in the first two chapters, Wesley struggled continuously with the need to balance and to integrate his commitment to the Church of England and his commitment to Methodism. Within the framework of a robust doctrine of providence, we can take Wesley at his word when he insists that the Methodists were complementary to the services of the Church of England. We can also better understand why, on the one hand, he refused to leave the Church of England; and on the other hand, he refused to leave the Methodists. If they were both the working of divine providence, then for Wesley to leave either one would have been tantamount to turning his back on the grace of God.

Finally, if this view of Wesley is correct, then the grace to which he felt himself responsible was more comprehensive than we have dared to think or imagine. As such, we can readily attribute whatever inconsistencies and tensions that remain to the moral dilemmas that inevitably arise when a robust doctrine of divine providence is combined with an equally robust form of covenantal Arminianism. Perceived this way, inconsistencies and tensions in Wesley's life and thought should not be smoothed over or ignored. Rather, they should be taken as a sign that John Wesley was someone for whom the manifold grace of God was constantly outstripping his capacity for joyful obedience, love and praise.

NOTES

INTRODUCTION

1. John Wesley, 'Preface' to 'Sermons on Several Occasions', §3, in *Sermons I*, ed. Albert C. Outler, vol. 1 of *The Bicentennial Edition of the Works of John Wesley* (Nashville, TN: Abingdon Press, 1976–), 104.
2. Ibid., §4, 104.
3. John Wesley, Letter to John Mason (13 January 1790), Letter DXXIX, in *The Works of John Wesley*, ed. Thomas Jackson, 3rd edn (London: Wesleyan Methodist Book Room, 1872; reprint, Kansas City, MO: Beacon Hill Press, 1986), 12:455.
4. John Wesley, 'A Word to a Freeholder' (1747), in *Works* (Jackson), 11:197–8.

CHAPTER ONE: SPREADING THE GOSPEL: METHODISM AND THE EVANGELICAL REVIVAL

1. See the section in the *Book of Common Prayer* entitled 'The Consecration of Bishops'. For priests and deacons, see the sections 'The Ordering of Priests' and 'The Ordering of Deacons'.
2. See 'The Solemnization of Matrimony' in the *Book of Common Prayer*.
3. Richard Hooker, *Of the Laws of Ecclesiastical Polity (1594–1662)*, in *Works*, ed. J. Keble, 7th edn (Oxford: Clarendron Press, 1888), 8.2.2.
4. The date is significant because it was a full 14 years after the Revolution. Suffice it to say, most English citizens, including Samuel, had come to accept the authority, if not the legitimacy, of William and Mary. Evidence for this fairly widespread acceptance lies in the fact that Jacobite sympathizers never could rouse enough support to constitute a serious threat (the Jacobites were those who desired the return of the Stuart line to the throne). For more on the Jacobites, including the '45 Rebellion, see Chapter Three.
5. Luke Tyerman, *The Life and Times of the Rev. Samuel Wesley, M.A., Rector of Epworth, and the Father of the Revs. John and Charles Wesley, the Founders of the Methodists* (London: Simpkin, Marshall & Co., 1866), p. 347.
6. An enthusiast is someone who claimed to answer directly to God. Because it was so easy for enthusiasts simply to appeal to God in order to justify disorderliness and insubordination within English society, they could be regarded as highly dangerous.

7. See especially Richard P. Heitzenrater, 'The Church of England and the Religious Societies', in *Mirror and Memory: Reflections on Early Methodism*, ed. Richard P. Heitzenrater (Nashville, TN: Kingswood Books, 1989), pp. 33–45.

8. William J. Abraham, *Wesley for Armchair Theologians* (Louisville, KY: Westminster John Knox Press, 2005), p. 5.

9. John Wesley, 4 March 1738, *Journal and Diaries I (1735–1738)*, ed. W. Reginald Ward and Richard P. Heitzenrater, vol. 18 of *The Bicentennial Edition of the Works of John Wesley* (Nashville, TN: Abingdon Press, 1976–), 228.

10. Ibid., 14 May 1738, 249–50.

11. At least one scholar has suggested that Methodist piety has over the years been reduced to the norm of Aldersgate. See Jean Miller Schmidt, ' "Strangely Warmed": The Place of Aldersgate in the Methodist Canon', in *Aldersgate Reconsidered*, ed. Randy Maddox (Nashville, TN: Kingswood Books, 1990), pp. 109–20.

12. For the best account of Wesley's spiritual and intellectual pilgrimage leading up to and just after Aldersgate, see Richard P. Heitzenrater, 'Great Expectations: Aldersgate and the Evidences of Genuine Christianity', in Heitzenrater, *Mirror and Memory*, pp. 106–49.

13. Frederick Dreyer, *The Genesis of Methodism* (Bethlehem, PA: Lehigh University Press, 1999), p. 13.

14. John Wesley, Letter to [The Revd. John Clayton?] (28 March 1739), in *Letters I (1721–1739)*, ed. Frank Baker, in *Works*, 25:616.

15. Wesley, 31 March 1739, *Journal and Diaries II (1738–1743)*, ed. W. Reginald Ward and Richard P. Heitzenrater, in *Works*, 19:46.

16. Richard P. Heitzenrater, *Wesley and the People Called Methodists* (Nashville, TN: Abingdon Press, 1995), p. 94.

17. For the extent of Wesley's travels at this time, see Henry D. Rack, *Reasonable Enthusiast: John Wesley and the Rise of Methodism* (London: Epworth Press, 1989), pp. 214–37.

18. For more on the '45 Rebellion and the accusations of Jacobitism, see Chapter Three.

19. As quoted in Heitzenrater, *Wesley and the People Called Methodists*, p. 214.

20. For more on this, see Chapter Three.

21. John Wesley, Letter to William Wilberforce (24 February 1791), in *The Letters of the Rev. John Wesley*, ed. John Telford (London: Epworth Press, 1931), 8:264–5.

22. See especially Cynthia Lynn Lyerly, *Methodism and the Southern Mind, 1770–1810* (New York: Oxford University Press, 1998); and Christine Leigh Heyrman, *Southern Cross: The Beginnings of the Bible Belt* (Chapel Hill, NC: University of North Carolina Press, 1997).

23. For more on this, see Jason E. Vickers, 'Christology', in *The Oxford Handbook of Methodist Studies*, ed. William J. Abraham and James Kirby (Oxford: Oxford University Press, forthcoming in 2009).

24. As quoted by Heitzenrater, *Wesley and the People Called Methodists*, p. 288.

25. As quoted by Heitzenrater, ibid., p. 303.

26. Wesley, Letter to Henry Moore (6 May 1788), in *Letters*, 8:58.

27. Wesley, Letter to Mr. [?] (31 October 1789), in *Letters*, 8:183.

28. John Wesley, 1 March 1791, in *The Journal of the Rev. John Wesley, A.M.*, ed. Nehemiah Curnock (London: R. Culley, 1909–1916), 8:138–44.

CHAPTER TWO: KEEPING TO THE CHURCH:
THE STABILIZATION OF ENGLISH SOCIETY

1. The popularity of this image can be seen in the title of Roy Hattersley's recent mass-market biography of Wesley, *The Life of John Wesley: A Brand from the Burning* (New York: Doubleday, 2003).

2. For a critical study of the reception history of Wesley's references to the heart and to heart religion, see especially Richard B. Steele, ed., *'Heart Religion' in the Methodist Tradition and Related Movements* (Lanham, MD: Scarecrow Press, 2001).

3. For more on Wesley's relationship to the state, see Chapter Three.

4. Frank Baker, *John Wesley and the Church of England* (Nashville, TN: Abingdon, 1970), p. 1 [italicized emphasis added].

5. Jeremy Gregory, '"In the Church I will live and die,"' in *Religious Identities in Britain, 1660–1832*, eds. William Gibson and Robert G. Ingram (Aldershot: Ashgate, 2005), p. 149.

6. John Wesley, Sermon 75, 'On Schism', II.17, in *Sermons III*, ed. Albert C. Outler, vol. 3 of *The Bicentennial Edition of the Works of John Wesley* (Nashville, TN: Abingdon Press, 1976–), 67.

7. John Wesley, Letter to Gilbert Boyce (22 May 1750), in *The Letters of the Rev. John Wesley*, ed. John Telford (London: Epworth Press, 1931), 3:36.

8. Wesley, Letter to Joseph Taylor (16 January 1783), in *Letters*, 7:163.

9. Wesley, Letter to Henry Moore (6 May 1788), in *Letters*, 8:58.

10. As quoted in Baker, *John Wesley*, p. 2.

11. Ibid. For the most positive appraisal of Wesley's relationship to the Church of England available to date, see Gregory, '"In the Church I will live and die."'

12. David Hempton, *The Religion of the People: Methodism and Popular Religion c. 1750–1900* (London: Routledge, 1996), p. 83.

13. Gregory, '"In the Church I will live and die,"' p. 150.

14. Maldwyn Edwards, 'John Wesley', in *A History of the Methodist Church in Great Britain*, ed. Rupert Davies and Gordon Rupp (London: Epworth, 1965), vol. 1: pp. 72–3.

15. Baker, *John Wesley*, pp. 2–3.

16. See especially Roy Porter, *The Creation of the Modern World: The Untold Story of the British Enlightenment* (New York: Norton, 2000); also see Peter Harrison, *'Religion' and the Religions in the English Enlightenment* (Cambridge: Cambridge University Press, 1990).

17. John Walsh, '"Methodism" and the Origins of English-Speaking Evangelicalism', in *Evangelicalism: Comparative Studies of Popular Protestantism in North America, the British Isles, and Beyond, 1700–1900*, ed. Mark A. Noll, David W. Bebbington and George A. Rawlyk (New York: Oxford University Press, 1994), p. 23.

18. Socinianism is the name for a rational form of Christianity linked to the life and work of Faustus Socinus in Poland. In the seventeenth century, Socinian publications, most notably the *Rakovian Catechism*, began to make their way into England. Unitarianism is the name for the rational form of Christianity in England that was directly influenced by Socinianism. For more on the origin, spread and influence of Socinianism and Unitarianism in England, see Jason

E. Vickers, *Invocation and Assent: The Making and Remaking of Trinitarian Theology* (Grand Rapids, MI: Eerdmans, 2008).

19. For example, see Stephen Taylor, 'Sir Robert Walpole, the Church of England, and the Quakers Tithe Bill of 1736', *Historical Journal* 28 (1985): 51–77.

20. See especially A. M. C. Waterman, 'The Nexus between Theology and Political Doctrine in Church and Dissent', in *Enlightenment and Religion: Rational Dissent in Eighteenth-Century Britain*, ed. Knud Haakonssen (New York: Cambridge University Press, 1996), pp. 193–218.

21. For the growing sense that natural philosophy could solve problems related to the navigation of the world, see William S. Babcock, 'The Commerce between the Mind and Things: A Re-shaping of the World in the Seventeenth Century', in *The Unbounded Community*, ed. William Caferro and Duncan G. Fisher (New York: Garland, 1996), pp. 163–86.

22. For the relationship between revealed religion and natural philosophy, see Peter Harrison, *The Bible, Protestantism, and the Rise of Natural Science* (New York: Cambridge University Press, 1998).

23. J. Wesley Bready, *England: Before and After Wesley: The Evangelical Revival and Social Reform* (New York: Harper and Brothers, 1938), p. 63.

24. Ibid., pp. 41–2.

25. As quoted in Gerald R. Cragg, *The Church and the Age of Reason, 1648–1789* (Grand Rapids, MI: Eerdmans, 1962), p. 125.

26. As quoted in Walsh, ' "Methodism" and the Origins', p. 24.

27. George Berkeley, *Discourse Addressed to Magistrates and Men in Authority* (Dublin: George Faulkner, 1738), p. 41.

28. See Markman Ellis, *The Coffee House: A Cultural History* (London: Orion, 2004). Also see Brian Cowan, *The Social Life of Coffee: The Emergence of the British Coffeehouse* (New Haven, CT: Yale University Press, 2005).

29. Walsh, ' "Methodism" and the Origins', p. 25.

30. Wesley, Sermon 102, 'Of Former Times', §20, in *Works*, 3:452; Sermon 106, 'On Faith', I.2, in *Works*, 3:494.

31. Wesley, Sermon 133, 'Death and Deliverance', §10, in *Works*, 4:210.

32. Wesley, Sermon 125, 'On a Single Eye', III.5, in *Works*, 4:128.

33. Leslie Stephen, *History of English Thought in the Eighteenth Century* (New York: Peter Smith, 1949), 2: pp. 411–13.

34. E. P. Thompson, 'Anthropology and the Discipline of Historical Context', *Midland History* 1, no. 3 (1972): 54.

35. Bready, *England: Before and After Wesley*, p. 200.

36. Scholars in this group include R. E. Brantley, Frederick Dreyer and David Bebbington.

37. Frederick Dreyer, 'A "Religious Society under Heaven": John Wesley and the Identity of Methodism', *Journal of British Studies* 25 (1986): 81.

38. As quoted by Dreyer, 'A "Religious Society under Heaven"', 82. Dreyer cites John Locke, *The Second Treatise on Civil Government and Letter Concerning Toleration*, ed. J. W. Gough (Oxford: Basil Blackwell, 1948), p. 129.

39. Dreyer, 'A "Religious Society under Heaven"', 79.

40. David W. Bebbington, *Evangelicalism in Modern Britain: A History from the 1730s to the 1980s* (London: Unwin Hyman, 1989), p. 53.

41. Ibid., 51–2; Wesley, Letter to Dr Thomas Rutherford (28 March 1768), in *Letters*, 5: 364.

42. Bebbington, *Evangelicalism in Modern Britain*, p. 57.

43. Ibid., p. 52.

44. Ibid., pp. 57–8.

45. Ibid., p. 60.

46. See Jeremy Gregory, *Restoration, Reformation, and Reform, 1660–1828: Archbishops of Canterbury and their Diocese* (Oxford: Clarendon Press, 2000), p. 1.

47. William J. Abraham suggests that scholars often underestimate the extent to which criticism of the established church reflects the English penchant for satire. In other words, it may be that the harshest and most sweeping criticisms, including the criticisms levied by John Wesley, were deliberate, over-the-top exaggerations for the purpose of making a point. This is not to say that the criticisms were not aimed at real problems, but simply that the problems might not have been as pervasive as the criticisms suggest. William J. Abraham, telephone conversation with author, 20 June 2008.

48. J. C. D. Clark, *English Society, 1660–1832: Religion, Ideology and Politics During the Ancien Regime*, 2nd edn (Cambridge: Cambridge University Press, 2000), p. 424.

49. Jeremy Gregory, 'The Eighteenth-Century Reformation: The Pastoral Task of Anglican Clergy after 1689', in *The Church of England, c. 1689–c. 1833: From Toleration to Tractarianism*, ed. John Walsh, Colin Haydon, and Stephen Taylor (Cambridge: Cambridge University Press, 1993), p. 68.

50. Gregory, *Restoration, Reformation, and Reform*, p. 181.

51. B. W. Young, *Religion and Enlightenment in Eighteenth Century England: Theological Debate from Locke to Burke* (Oxford: Clarendon Press, 1998), p. 21.

52. Cragg, *The Church and the Age of Reason*, p. 120.

53. One must be careful, however, not to exaggerate the importance of the Corporation and Test Acts. See John Walsh and Stephen Taylor, 'The Church and Anglicanism in the "Long" Eighteenth Century', in *The Church of England, c. 1689–c. 1833: From Toleration to Tractarianism*, ed. John Walsh, Colin Haydon, and Stephen Taylor (Cambridge: Cambridge University Press, 1993), pp. 16–17.

54. Clark, *English Society*, p. 361.

55. Cragg, pp. 133–4.

56. Walsh and Taylor, 'The Church and Anglicanism', p. 57.

57. This has recently taken place in the field of theology, as evidenced by the sudden creation of new journals and book series in 'political theology'.

58. For a much needed corrective to the tendency among Wesley studies experts to read Wesley in ways that are tone-deaf to the intimate connection between politics and religion in eighteenth-century England, see Theodore R. Weber, *Politics in the Order of Salvation: Transforming Wesleyan Political Ethics* (Nashville, TN: Kingswood Books, 2001).

59. Waterman, 'The Nexus Between Theology and Political Doctrine', p. 195.

60. Clark, *English Society*, p. 327.

61. Ibid., p. 29. For more on this, see Owen Chadwick, *The Secularization of the European Mind in the Nineteenth Century* (Cambridge: Cambridge University

Press, 1975); and Jane Shaw, *Miracles in Enlightenment England* (New Haven, CT: Yale University Press, 2006).

62. For Wesley's belief in the Trinity, see Geoffrey Wainwright's chapter on 'Why Wesley was a Trinitarian' in *Methodists in Dialogue*, ed. G. Wainwright (Nashville, TN: Kingswood Books, 1995), pp. 261–76. For the frequency with which Wesley received the sacraments, see Trevor Dearing, *Wesleyan and Tractarian Worship* (London: Epworth Press, 1966).

63. Gregory, *Restoration, Reformation, and Reform*, p. 226.

64. For example, Theodore W. Jennings says that Wesley's involvement in field preaching and use of lay leaders was a 'departure' from the 'settled polity' of the established church. See Theodore W. Jennings Jr, *Good News to the Poor: John Wesley's Evangelical Economics* (Nashville, TN: Abingdon Press, 1990), p. 200.

65. Gregory, ' "In the Church I will live and die," ' p. 162. Gregory notes that, as bishop, Horne allowed Wesley to preach in his diocese of Norwich.

66. See especially Richard P. Heitzenrater, 'The Church of England and the Religious Societies', in *Mirror and Memory: Reflections on Early Methodism*, ed. Richard P. Heitzenrater (Nashville, TN: Kingswood Books, 1989), pp. 33–45; also see Henry Rack, 'Religious Societies and the Origin of Methodism', *Journal of Ecclesiastical History* 38 (1987): 583–95.

67. See Gregory, ' "In the Church I will live and die," ' p. 163.

68. See Elie Halevy, *The Birth of Methodism in England*, trans. and ed. Bernard Semmel (Chicago, IL: University of Chicago Press, 1971). For responses to the Halevy thesis, see *Religion and Revolution in Early-Industrial England: The Halevy Thesis and Its Critics*, ed. Gerald Wayne Olsen (Lanham, MD: University Press of America, 1990).

69. John Wesley, 'The Principles of a Methodist Farther Explained' (1746), III.1, in *The Methodist Societies: History, Nature, and Design*, ed. Rupert E. Davies, in *Works*, 9:185.

70. As with the parish clergy, there were more than a few bishops who were favourably disposed toward Wesley and the Methodists, including John Potter, Thomas Secker, Beilby Porteus and the aforementioned George Horne. For more on these bishops and their support of Wesley, see Gregory, ' "In the Church I will live and die," ' pp. 173–4.

71. Henry D. Rack, *Reasonable Enthusiast: John Wesley and the Rise of Methodism* (Philadelphia, PA: Trinity Press International, 1989), p. 302. Heitzenrater offers a slightly different list of priorities – namely, God, Church, and Methodism. He suggests that Wesley was simply not as clear on the order. See Richard P. Heitzenrater, *Wesley and the People Called Methodists* (Nashville, TN: Abingdon Press, 1995), p. 199.

72. For example, Randy Maddox contends that 'responsible grace' is the 'orienting concern' of John Wesley's theology. See Randy Maddox, *Responsible Grace: John Wesley's Practical Theology* (Nashville, TN: Kingswood Books, 1994).

73. John Wesley, 'Reasons Against a Separation from the Church of England' (1758), I.12, in *Works*, 9:336.

74. Ibid., III.4–5, 9:340.

75. See especially Shaw, *Miracles in Enlightenment England*.

76. While it is possible to associate Wesley more with popular culture than with the intellectual and social elite of eighteenth-century England, it is difficult to do

so with Bishop Warburton unless one is willing to limit intellectual and social status to liberal progressivism, denying such status not only to Warburton but to Edmund Burke as well.

77. Wesley, Letter to James Clark (3 July 1756), in *Letters*, 3:182.
78. For more on this, see Jason E. Vickers, 'Christology', in *The Oxford Handbook of Methodist Studies*, ed. William J. Abraham and James Kirby (Oxford: Oxford University Press, forthcoming in 2009).
79. John Wesley, 'The Character of a Methodist' (1742), §1, in *Works*, 9:34.
80. At the outset of the Methodist movement, Wesley asked, 'Are we members of the Church of England?' He answered his own question, saying, 'First, then, let us observe her laws, and then the bye-laws of our Society.' Wesley, Letter to James Hutton (1 December 1738), in *Letters*, 1:276. See also Wesley, Sermon 101, 'The Duty of Constant Communion', in *Works*, 3:427–39.
81. Wesley, Letter to James Knox (30 May 1765), in *Letters*, 4:303 [italicized emphasis added]. For more on Wesley's Anglican theology, see Chapter Four.
82. For example, Geoffrey Wainwright suggests that, while American Methodism would pick up on and retain one half of Wesley's political theology, namely, the injunction to 'think and let think', it would come largely to ignore the other half, most notably the commitment to the Trinity. See Wainwright, 'Why Wesley was a Trinitarian', p. 262.
83. John Wesley, 'Principles of a Methodist Farther Explained' III.9, in *Works*, 9:195 [italicized emphasis is Wesley's].

CHAPTER THREE: HONOURING THE KING:
THE POLITICS OF DIVINE RIGHT

1. For a reading of Wesley as a Puritan, see Robert C. Monk, *John Wesley: His Puritan Heritage, a Study of the Christian Life* (London: Epworth Press, 1966).
2. Maldwyn Edwards, *John Wesley and the Eighteenth Century: A Study of His Social and Political Influence* (London: Allen & Unwin, 1933), p. 13.
3. In fact, as we will see later, eighteenth-century England was a constitutional monarchy in which Parliament played a crucial role in government. In this sense, it is more apt to refer to an oligarchy than to a monarchy.
4. William Warren Sweet, 'John Wesley, Tory', *Methodist Quarterly Review* 71 (1922): 255–6.
5. Ibid., 262.
6. John Wesley, 5 March 1744, *Journal and Diaries III (1743–1754)*, ed. W. Reginald Ward and Richard P. Heitzenrater, vol. 20 of *The Bicentennial Edition of the Works of John Wesley* (Nashville, TN: Abingdon Press, 1976–), 16; hereafter cited as *Works* (Bicentennial).
7. John Wesley, Letter to the Mayor of Cork (27 May 1750), in *The Letters of the Rev. John Wesley*, ed. John Telford (London: Epworth Press, 1931), 3:38.
8. John Wesley, 'Free Thoughts on the Present State of Public Affairs' (1768), in *The Works of John Wesley*, ed. Thomas Jackson, 3rd edn (London: Wesleyan Methodist Book Room, 1872; reprint, Kansas City, MO: Beacon Hill Press, 1986), 11:23, 28; hereafter cited as *Works* (Jackson).
9. Ibid., 11:48, 52.

10. John Wesley, Letter to William Legge, the Earl of Dartmouth, Secretary of State for the Colonies (14 June 1775), in *Letters*, 6:156.
11. Leon O. Hynson, 'John Wesley and Political Reality', *Methodist History* 12 (1973): 38. Hynson cites George M. Trevelyan, *England under the Stuarts* (London: Methuen and Co., 1904), pp. 451–60.
12. Bernard Semmel, *The Methodist Revolution* (New York: Basic Books, 1973), p. 93.
13. Ibid., p. 63.
14. Ibid., p. 70.
15. Frederick Dreyer, 'Edmund Burke and John Wesley: The Legacy of Locke', in *Religion, Secularization, and Political Thought: Thomas Hobbes to J. S. Mill*, ed. James E. Cummings (London: Routledge, 1989), p. 118.
16. Sweet consistently refers to Wesley simply as a Tory and not as a Jacobite or Nonjuror. In his biography of the early Wesley, V. H. H. Green goes so far as to deny that Wesley was ever 'a Jacobite in fact'. See V. H. H. Green, *The Young Mr. Wesley* (New York: St. Martin's Press, 1961), p. 78.
17. Semmel, *The Methodist Revolution*, p. 57.
18. Leon O. Hynson, 'Human Liberty as Divine Right: A Study in the Political Maturation of John Wesley', *Journal of Church and State* 25 (1983): 58.
19. Robert Walmsley, 'John Wesley's Parents: Quarrel and Reconciliation', *Proceedings of the Wesley Historical Society* 29 (1953): 50–7. The sources for this story are varied, including letters from Susanna Wesley, written recollections by John Wesley and recollections recorded by acquaintances of John Wesley, most notably Adam Clarke. Walsmley's essay cites most of the important sources.
20. Maximin Piette, *John Wesley in the Evolution of Protestantism* (London: Sheed & Ward, 1937), p. 290.
21. Hynson, 'Human Liberty as Divine Right', 59.
22. Ibid., 67–8.
23. Ibid., 69.
24. See especially Frank Baker, 'Methodism and the '45 Rebellion', *London Quarterly and Holborn Review* 172 (1947): 325–33.
25. Semmel, *The Methodist Revolution*, p. 58.
26. Interested readers can access all 12 of Wesley's major political treatises in *Works* (Jackson), vol. XI.
27. One should here recall that Wesley's grandfather was evicted from his livings and imprisoned for being a dissenter.
28. John Wesley, 'Thoughts upon Liberty' (1772), §17, in *Works* (Jackson), 11:39.
29. Ibid.
30. John Wesley, 'A Calm Address to the Inhabitants of England' (1777), §21, in *Works* (Jackson), 11:137.
31. Wesley, Letter to William Legge (14 June 1775), in *Letters*, 6:156.
32. Wesley, 'Calm Address to the Inhabitants', §20, 11:136.
33. Wesley, 'Thoughts upon Slavery' (1774), IV.3, in *Works* (Jackson), 11:70.
34. Ibid., V.6, 11:79.
35. Richard P. Heitzenrater has stressed that Wesley was close to his mother and father alike. See his *The Elusive Mr. Wesley*, 2nd edn (Nashville, TN: Abingdon Press, 2003), pp. 219–20.

36. Frank O'Gorman, *British Conservatism: Conservative Thought from Burke to Thatcher* (London: Longman, 1986), p. 11.

37. Wesley, 'Free Thoughts on Public Affairs', 11:27.

38. David Hempton, *Methodism and Politics in British Society, 1750–1850* (Stanford, CA: Stanford University Press, 1984), p. 45. Henry Sacheverell (1674–1724) was notorious in the late seventeenth and early eighteenth centuries for arguing that the Whig ministry had neglected the church, making him a hero to Tories. He was eventually put on trial in 1710, and his conviction and suspension led to the 'Sacheverell Riots', which in turn led to the passing of the Riot Act of 1714.

39. Harry L. Howard in 'John Wesley: Tory or Democrat?' *Methodist History* 31 (1992): 45. For an older but still classic overview of this topic, see John Neville Figgis, *The Divine Right of Kings* (Cambridge: Cambridge University Press, 1896).

40. David Hempton, *The Religion of the People: Methodism and Popular Religion c. 1750–1900* (London: Routledge, 1996), pp. 81–2.

41. Among other things, what makes J. C. D. Clark's work so important is that he allows individuals like John Wesley to shape our understanding of the eighteenth century. See especially his *English Society, 1660–1832: Religion, Ideology and Politics During the Ancien Regime*, 2nd edn (Cambridge: Cambridge University Press, 2000), pp. 284–99.

42. Hempton, *Religion of the People*, pp. 79–80. Hempton goes on to say of Wesley, 'His Toryism, though tinged with . . . anti-Whig radicalism . . . was never allowed to spill over into overt support for the Jacobite cause' (p. 82).

43. Ibid., p. 80.

44. Ibid., p. 82.

45. Theodore W. Jennings, *Good News to the Poor: John Wesley's Evangelical Economics* (Nashville, TN: Abingdon Press, 1990), p. 200.

46. Nathan O. Hatch first argued this thesis in his well-known and oft-cited essay, 'The Puzzle of American Methodism', *Church History* 63 (1994): 175–89. For a book length version of Hatch's original thesis, see John Wigger, *Taking Heaven by Storm: Methodism and the Rise of Popular Christianity in America* (New York: Oxford University Press, 1998).

47. In some quarters of American Methodism, there exists a strong sense that the American Methodist tradition lost its connection to Wesley somewhere in the nineteenth century. For some, this is a cause for celebration. For others, the way forward for Methodism consists partly in a rediscovery of Wesley. The question here, of course, is whether some people are rediscovering Wesley as they want him to be rather than as he was. As we will see up ahead, my own judgement is that the emphasis on Wesley's concern for natural rights and human liberty is misleading at best. For the argument that American Methodism lost its connection with Wesley, see especially Randy L. Maddox, 'Respected Founder/ Neglected Guide: The Role of Wesley in American Methodist Theology', *Methodist History* 37 (1999): 71–88.

48. Jennings, *Good News to the Poor*, p. 48.

49. Theodore R. Weber, *Politics in the Order of Salvation* (Nashville, TN: Kingswood Books, 2001).

50. Ibid., p. 30.

51. John Wesley, Sermon 150, 'Hypocrisy in Oxford' [English], I.11, in *Sermons IV*, ed. Albert C. Outler, in *Works* (Bicentennial), 4:399.
52. John Wesley, 'The Doctrine of Original Sin, According to Scripture, Reason, and Experience' (1757), Part I, II.11, in *Works* (Jackson), 9:224.
53. John Wesley, as reported in the *Leeds Intelligencer*, 4 May 1790.
54. Weber, *Politics in the Order of Salvation*, p. 30.
55. John Wesley, 'A Word to a Freeholder' (1747), in *Works* (Jackson), 11:197–8; Weber quotes this passage in his *Politics in the Order of Salvation*, pp. 30–1.
56. Weber, *Politics in the Order of Salvation*, p. 304.
57. Ibid.
58. John Wesley, Sermon 60, 'The General Deliverance', I.1, in *Sermons II*, ed. Albert C. Outler, in *Works* (Bicentennial), 2:439 [emphasis original].
59. Weber, *Politics in the Order of Salvation*, p. 307.
60. We will say more about this in the next chapter.
61. Weber, *Politics in the Order of Salvation*, p. 309.
62. Ibid., p. 311.
63. John Wesley, 'A Calm Address to Our American Colonies' (1775), §4, in *Works* (Jackson), 11:83 [italicized emphasis added].
64. Weber, *Politics in the Order of Salvation*, p. 310 [emphasis original].
65. Ibid., p. 315.
66. Ibid., p. 318 [emphasis original].
67. Ibid., p. 305.
68. Ibid., p. 321.
69. John Wesley, Sermon 98, 'On Visiting the Sick', III.7, in *Sermons III*, ed. Albert C. Outler, in *Works* (Bicentennial), 396.
70. Weber, *Politics in the Order of Salvation*, p. 339.
71. Wesley, 'Thoughts upon Liberty', §16, 11:37–8.
72. Weber, *Politics in the Order of Salvation*, pp. 323–4 [emphasis original].
73. For a thorough analysis of the evidence of Wesley's anti-Catholic sentiments, see especially Hempton, *Methodism and Politics*, pp. 34–43. Hempton explicitly denies that the 'Letter to a Roman Catholic' was 'typical' of Wesley's views on Catholicism (p. 36).
74. Weber, *Politics in the Order of Salvation*, p. 330.
75. John Wesley, Letter to the Printer of the *Public Advertiser* (12 January 1780), in *Letters*, 6:371.
76. D. Stephen Long, *John Wesley's Moral Theology: The Quest for God and Goodness* (Nashville, TN: Kingswood Books, 2005), p. 236.
77. Weber, *Politics in the Order of Salvation*, p. 35.
78. Ibid., pp. 200–1.
79. Ibid., p. 35.

CHAPTER FOUR: LOVING GOD: A THEOLOGY OF JOYFUL OBEDIENCE

1. For example, see Robert C. Monk, *John Wesley: His Puritan Heritage, A Study of the Christian Life* (London: Epworth Press, 1966).
2. Paul Bayne, *Christian Letters* (London: Thomas Dawson, 1637), p. 340. For more on covenant theology in early Puritanism, see John von Rohr, 'Covenant

and Assurance in Early English Puritanism', *Church History* 34 (1965): 195–203.

3. Gordon Rupp, *Religion in England, 1688–1791* (Oxford: Clarendon Press, 1986), p. 343.
4. See the posthumously published work by Walker entitled *The Covenant of Grace, in Nine Sermons* (London, 1788).
5. Nicholas Tyacke, 'Puritanism, Arminianism and Counter-Revolution', in *Origins of the English Civil War*, ed. Conrad Russell (New York: Macmillan, 1973), p. 145.
6. See Phillip Schaff, *Creeds of Christendom* (New York: Harper, 1919), vol.3: p. 551.
7. The Remonstrant Confession of Faith 9.1 (1622), quoted in Jaroslav Pelikan, *The Christian Tradition: A History of the Development of Doctrine* (Chicago, IL: University of Chicago Press, 1984), vol. 4: p. 240.
8. Ibid., 2.9, quoted in Pelikan, *The Christian Tradition*, vol. 4: p. 233.
9. Ibid., 9.1, quoted in Pelikan, *The Christian Tradition*, vol. 4: p. 235.
10. See chapter eight in Peter A. Lillback, *The Binding of God: Calvin's Role in the Development of Covenant Theology* (Grand Rapids, MI: Baker Academic, 2000).
11. Arminianism in seventeenth-century England expressed itself primarily in the rule of faith controversy. For more on this, see chapter two in Jason E. Vickers, *Invocation and Assent: The Making and Remaking of Trinitarian Theology* (Grand Rapids, MI: Eerdmans, 2008).
12. Pelikan, *The Christian Tradition*, vol. 4: p. 236.
13. John Wesley, Letter to Mary Bishop (7 February 1778), in *The Letters of the Rev. John Wesley*, ed. John Telford (London: Epworth Press, 1931), 6:297.
14. John Wesley, Sermon 35, 'The Law Established Through Faith, Discourse I', II.3, in *Sermons II*, ed. Albert C. Outler, vol. 2 of *The Bicentennial Edition of the Works of John Wesley* (Nashville, TN: Abingdon Press, 1976–), 27.
15. Wesley, Sermon 34, 'The Original, Nature, Properties, and Use of the Law', III.7, in *Works*, 2:13.
16. Ibid., II.3, 2:9.
17. Ibid., III.1, 2:10.
18. Ibid., I.3–4, 2:7.
19. Wesley, Sermon 60, 'The General Deliverance', I.2, in *Works*, 2:439.
20. For an example of Wesley's use of this expression, see Sermon 45, 'The New Birth', I.1, in *Works*, 2:188. Wesley also spoke of the political image of God, which referred to God's creating humankind to be caretakers of the earth.
21. Wesley, 'The General Deliverance', I.1, in *Works*, 2:438–9.
22. John Wesley, Sermon 141, 'The Image of God', I.3, in *Sermons IV*, ed. Albert C. Outler, in *Works*, 4:295.
23. Wesley, 'The Original, Nature, Properties, and Use of the Law', I.4, in *Works*, 2:7.
24. For more on the perception that Arminianism implies a doctrine of free will, see Roger E. Olson, *Arminian Theology: Myths and Realities* (Downers Grove, IL: IVP, 2006), pp. 137–57.
25. John Wesley, Sermon 26, 'Upon our Lord's Sermon on the Mount, Discourse the Sixth', III.13, in *Sermons I*, ed. Albert C. Outler, in *Works*, 1:586.
26. Wesley, 'The Original, Nature, Properties, and Use of the Law', I.4, in *Works*, 2:7.

27. Wesley, Sermon 6, 'The Righteousness of Faith', §1, in *Works*, 1:202–3.
28. Albert C. Outler, 'An Introductory Comment' to John Wesley, Sermon 110, 'Free Grace', in *Sermons III*, ed. Albert C. Outler, in *Works*, 3:542.
29. Wesley, Sermon 110, 'Free Grace', §21, in *Works*, 3:553.
30. Wesley, Sermon 1, 'Salvation by Faith', I.4–5, in *Works*, 1:120–1 (emphasis original).
31. Wesley, Sermon 35, 'The Law Established Through Faith, Discourse I', II.3–4, in *Works*, 2:27 (emphasis original).
32. Wesley, 'The New Birth', II.4, in *Works*, 2:192.
33. Ibid., 2:192–3.
34. Ibid., 2:193.
35. See chapter three in Vickers, *Invocation and Assent*.
36. For the depth of the problem of assurance in Protestant theology, see Randall Zachman, *The Assurance of Faith: Conscience in the Theology of Martin Luther and John Calvin* (Louisville, KY: Westminster John Knox Press, 2005).
37. See chapter two in Vickers, *Invocation and Assent*.
38. Wesley, Sermon 7, 'The Way to the Kingdom', I.5–6, in *Works*, 1:220–1 (emphasis original).
39. Wesley, Sermon 11, 'The Witness of the Spirit, Discourse II', II.6, in *Works*, 1:288.
40. Ibid., II.7, 1:288.
41. Wesley, Sermon 10, 'The Witness of the Spirit, Discourse I' I.4, in *Works*, 1:272.
42. Wesley, 'The Witness of the Spirit, II', II.7, in *Works*, 1:288.
43. Ibid., III.5, 1:290.
44. Ibid., V.1, 1:296.
45. Ibid., V.4, 1:298.
46. Ibid., V.3, 1:297.
47. Among the few who had an equally robust doctrine of the Holy Spirit was John's younger brother Charles. For more on Charles Wesley's doctrine of the Holy Spirit, see Jason E. Vickers, 'Charles Wesley's Doctrine of the Holy Spirit: A Vital Resource for the Renewal of Methodism', *Asbury Journal* 61:1 (Spring 2006), 47–60.
48. Wesley, Sermon 16, 'The Means of Grace', I.1, in *Works*, 1:378.
49. Ibid., II.1, 1:381 (emphasis original).
50. Ibid., The context makes it clear that the 'we' in 'we believe' refers to the Church of England.
51. Ibid., II.2, 1:381.
52. Some theologians discern a distinction in Wesley's theology between the means of grace in connection with justification and the means of grace in connection with sanctification. For example, see Randy Maddox, *Responsible Grace: John Wesley's Practical Theology* (Nashville, TN: Kingswood Books, 1994), pp. 192–229.
53. Wesley, Sermon 69, 'The Imperfection of Human Knowledge', III.5, in *Works*, 2:584.
54. John Wesley, Letter to Charles Wesley (September 1762), in *The Letters of the Rev. John Wesley*, ed. John Telford (London: Epworth Press, 1931), 4:187.
55. Ibid.
56. Romans 5.8.

57. For Sherlock, Wallis, and Stillingfleet's attempts to do so, see chapters three through five in Vickers, *Invocation and Assent*.
58. Wesley, Sermon 55, 'On the Trinity', §4, in *Works*, 2:378.
59. Wesley, Letter to Miss March (3 August 1771), in *Letters*, 5:270.
60. Wesley, 'On the Trinity', §17, in *Works*, 2:385.
61. For more on this, see chapter one in Catherine Mowry LaCugna, *God For Us: The Trinity and the Christian Life* (New York: HarperOne, 1993).
62. Wesley, Letter to Miss March (26 April 1777), in *Letters*, 6:263.
63. The testimonies of early Methodists regarding their religious experiences remain a grossly neglected area of study.
64. Wesley, Sermon 12, 'The Witness of Our Own Spirit', §20, in *Works*, 1:312 (emphasis original).
65. Theodore R. Weber, *Politics in the Order of Salvation* (Nashville, TN: Kingswood Books, 2001), p. 35.
66. Ibid., pp. 200–1.
67. Ibid., p. 35.

CONCLUSION

1. John Wesley, 'A Word to a Freeholder' (1747), in *The Works of John Wesley*, ed. Thomas Jackson, 3rd edn (London: Wesleyan Methodist Book Room, 1872; reprint, Kansas City, MO: Beacon Hill Press, 1986), 11:197.
2. John Wesley, Letter to Walter Churchey (25 June 1777), Letter CCCCXCII, *Works* 12:435.

BIBLIOGRAPHY

PRIMARY SOURCES

The Book of Common Prayer and Administration of the Sacraments and Other Rites and Ceremonies of the Church (New York: D. Appleton & Co., 1870).

Wesley, John. 'Preface' to 'Sermons on Several Occasions', §3, in *Sermons I*, ed. Albert C. Outler, vol. 1 of *The Bicentennial Edition of the Works of John Wesley* (Nashville, TN: Abingdon Press, 1976–), 104.

Wesley, John, Sermon 75, 'On Schism', II.17, in *Sermons III*, ed. Albert C. Outler, vol. 3 of *The Bicentennial Edition of the Works of John Wesley* (Nashville, TN: Abingdon Press, 1976–), 67.

Wesley, John. 4 March 1738, *Journal and Diaries I (1735–1738)*, ed. W. Reginald Ward and Richard P. Heitzenrater, vol. 18 of *The Bicentennial Edition of the Works of John Wesley* (Nashville, TN: Abingdon Press, 1976–), 228.

Wesley, John. *The Bicentennial Edition of the Works of John Wesley*, ed. Frank Baker and Richard P. Heitzenrater (Nashville, TN: Abingdon Press, 1976.

Wesley, John. *The Journal of the Rev. John Wesley, A.M.*, ed. Nehemiah Curnock (London: R. Culley, 1909–1916).

Wesley, John. *The Letters of the Rev. John Wesley*, ed. John Telford (London: Epworth Press, 1931).

Wesley, John. *The Works of John Wesley*, ed. Thomas Jackson, 3rd edn (London: Wesleyan Methodist Book Room, 1872; reprint, Kansas City, MO: Beacon Hill Press, 1986).

SECONDARY SOURCES

Abraham, William J. *Wesley for Armchair Theologians.* (Louisville, KY: Westminster John Knox Press, 2005).

Babcock, William S. 'The Commerce between the Mind and Things: A Re-shaping of the World in the Seventeenth Century', in *The Unbounded Community*, ed. W. Caferro and D.G. Fisher (New York: Garland, 1996), pp. 163–86.

Baker, Frank. *John Wesley and the Church of England.* (Nashville, TN: Abingdon, 1970).

Baker, Frank. 'Methodism and the '45 Rebellion', *London Quarterly and Holborn Review* 172 (1947): 325–33.

Bayne, Paul. *Christian Letters*. (London: Thomas Dawson, 1637).

Bebbington, David W. *Evangelicalism in Modern Britain: A History from the 1730s to the 1980s* (London: Unwin Hyman, 1989).

Berkeley, George. *Discourse Addressed to Magistrates and Men in Authority* (Dublin: George Faulkner, 1738).

Bready J. Wesley. *England: Before and After Wesley: The Evangelical Revival and Social Reform* (New York: Harper and Brothers, 1938).

Chadwick, Owen. *The Secularization of the European Mind in the Nineteenth Century* (Cambridge: Cambridge University Press, 1975).

Clark, J. C. D. (2000), *English Society, 1660–1832: Religion, Ideology and Politics During the Ancien Regime*, 2nd edn (Cambridge: Cambridge University Press, 2000).

Cowan, Brian. *The Social Life of Coffee: The Emergence of the British Coffeehouse* (New Haven, CT: Yale University Press, 2005).

Cragg, Gerald R. *The Church and the Age of Reason, 1648–1789* (Grand Rapids, MI: Eerdmans, 1962).

Dearing, Trevor. *Wesleyan and Tractarian Worship* (London: Epworth Press, 1966).

Dreyer, Frederick. (1986), 'A "Religious Society under Heaven": John Wesley and the Identity of Methodism', *Journal of British Studies* 25 (1986): 81.

Dreyer, Frederick. 'Edmund Burke and John Wesley: The Legacy of Locke', in *Religion, Secularization, and Political Thought: Thomas Hobbes to J. S. Mill*, ed. James E. Cummings (London: Routledge, 1989), p. 118.

Dreyer, Frederick. *The Genesis of Methodism* (Bethlehem, PA: Lehigh University Press, 1999).

Edwards, Maldwyn. *John Wesley and the Eighteenth Century: A Study of His Social and Political Influence* (London: Allen & Unwin, 1933).

Edwards, Maldwyn. 'John Wesley', in *A History of the Methodist Church in Great Britain*, ed. Rupert Davies and Gordon Rupp (London: Epworth, 1965), vol. 1: pp. 72–3.

Ellis, Markman. *The Coffee House: A Cultural History* (London: Orion, 2004).

Figgis, John Neville. *The Divine Right of Kings* (Cambridge: Cambridge University Press, 1896).

Green, V. H. H. *The Young Mr. Wesley* (New York: St Martin's Press, 1961).

Gregory, Jeremy. 'The Eighteenth-Century Reformation: The Pastoral Task of Anglican Clergy after 1689', in *The Church of England, c. 1689–c. 1833: From Toleration to Tractarianism*, ed. John Walsh, Colin Haydon, and Stephen Taylor (Cambridge: Cambridge University Press, 1993), p. 68.

Gregory, Jeremy. *Restoration, Reformation, and Reform, 1660–1828: Archbishops of Canterbury and their Diocese* (Oxford: Clarendon Press, 2000).

Gregory, Jeremy. '"In the Church I will live and die,"' in *Religious Identities in Britain, 1660–1832*, eds. William Gibson and Robert G. Ingram (Aldershot: Ashgate, 2005). p. 149.

Halevy, Elie. *The Birth of Methodism in England*, trans. and ed. Bernard Semmel (Chicago, IL: University of Chicago Press, 1971).

Harrison, Peter. *'Religion' and the Religions in the English Enlightenment* (Cambridge: Cambridge University Press, 1990).

Harrison, Peter. *The Bible, Protestantism, and the Rise of Natural Science* (New York: Cambridge University Press, 1998).

Hatch, Nathan O. 'The Puzzle of American Methodism', *Church History* 63 (1994): 175–89.

Hattersley, Roy. *The Life of John Wesley: A Brand from the Burning* (New York: Doubleday, 2003).

Heitzenrater, Richard P. *Wesley and the People Called Methodists* (Nashville, TN: Abingdon Press, 1995).

Heitzenrater, Richard P. *The Elusive Mr. Wesley*, 2nd edn (Nashville, TN: Abingdon Press, 2003).

Heitzenrater, Richard P. (ed.). *Mirror and Memory: Reflections on Early Methodism* (Nashville, TN: Kingswood Books, 1989).

Hempton, David. *Methodism and Politics in British Society, 1750–1850* (Stanford, CA: Stanford University Press, 1984).

Hempton, David. *The Religion of the People: Methodism and Popular Religion c. 1750–1900* (London: Routledge, 1996).

Heyrman, Christine Leigh. *Southern Cross: The Beginnings of the Bible Belt* (Chapel Hill, NC: University of North Carolina Press, 1997).

Hooker, Richard. *Of the Laws of Ecclesiastical Polity (1594–1662)*, in *Works*, ed. J. Keble, 7th edn (Oxford: Clarendon Press, 1888), 8.2.2.

Howard, Harry L. 'John Wesley: Tory or Democrat?' *Methodist History* 31 (1992): 45.

Hynson, Leon O. 'John Wesley and Political Reality', *Methodist History* 12 (1973): 38.

Hynson, Leon O. 'Human Liberty as Divine Right: A Study in the Political Maturation of John Wesley', *Journal of Church and State* 25 (1983): 58.

Jennings, Theodore W. Jr. *Good News to the Poor: John Wesley's Evangelical Economics* (Nashville, TN: Abingdon Press, 1990).

LaCugna, Catherine Mowry. *God For Us: The Trinity and the Christian Life* (New York: HarperOne, 1993).

Lillback, Peter A. *The Binding of God: Calvin's Role in the Development of Covenant Theology* (Grand Rapids, MI: Baker Academic, 2000).

Locke, John. *The Second Treatise on Civil Government and Letter Concerning Toleration*, ed. J. W. Gough (Oxford: Basil Blackwell, 1948).

Long, D. Stephen. *John Wesley's Moral Theology: The Quest for God and Goodness* (Nashville, TN: Kingswood Books, 2005).

Lyerly, Cynthia Lynn. *Methodism and the Southern Mind, 1770–1810* (New York: Oxford University Press, 1998).

Maddox, Randy. *Responsible Grace: John Wesley's Practical Theology* (Nashville, TN: Kingswood Books, 1994).

Monk, Robert C. *John Wesley: His Puritan Heritage, a Study of the Christian Life* (London: Epworth Press, 1966).

O'Gorman, Frank. *British Conservatism: Conservative Thought from Burke to Thatcher* (London: Longman, 1986).

Olsen, Gerald Wayne (ed.) *Religion and Revolution in Early-Industrial England: The Halevy Thesis and Its Critics* (Lanham, MD: University Press of America, 1990).

Olson, Roger E. *Arminian Theology: Myths and Realities* (Downers Grove, IL: IVP, 2006).

Pelikan, Jaroslav. *The Christian Tradition: A History of the Development of Doctrine* (Chicago, IL: University of Chicago Press, 1984).

Piette, Maximin. *John Wesley in the Evolution of Protestantism* (London: Sheed & Ward, 1937).

Porter, Roy. *The Creation of the Modern World: The Untold Story of the British Enlightenment* (New York: Norton, 2000).

Rack, Henry D. 'Religious Societies and the Origin of Methodism', *Journal of Ecclesiastical History* 38 (1987): 583–95.

Rack, Henry D. *Reasonable Enthusiast: John Wesley and the Rise of Methodism* (London: Epworth Press, 1989).

Rack, Henry D. *Reasonable Enthusiast: John Wesley and the Rise of Methodism* (Philadelphia, PA: Trinity Press International, 1989).

Rupp, Gordon. *Religion in England, 1688–1791* (Oxford: Clarendon Press, 1986).

Schaff, Phillip. *Creeds of Christendom* (New York: Harper, 1919).

Schmidt, Jean Miller. ' "Strangely Warmed": The Place of Aldersgate in the Methodist Canon', in *Aldersgate Reconsidered*, ed. Randy Maddox (Nashville, TN: Kingswood Books, 1990), pp. 109–20.

Semmel, Bernard. *The Methodist Revolution* (New York: Basic Books, 1973).

Shaw, Jane. *Miracles in Enlightenment England* (New Haven, CT: Yale University Press, 2006).

Steele, Richard B. (ed.). *'Heart Religion' in the Methodist Tradition and Related Movements* (Lanham, MD: Scarecrow Press, 2001).

Stephen, Leslie. *History of English Thought in the Eighteenth Century* (New York: Peter Smith, 1949).

Sweet, William Warren. 'John Wesley, Tory', *Methodist Quarterly Review* 71 (1922): 255–6.

Taylor, Stephen. 'Sir Robert Walpole, the Church of England, and the Quakers Tithe Bill of 1736', *Historical Journal* 28 (1985): 51–77.

Thompson, E. P. 'Anthropology and the Discipline of Historical Context', *Midland History* 1: no. 3 (1972): 54.

Trevelyan, George M. *England under the Stuarts* (London: Methuen and Co., 1904).

Tyacke, Nicholas. 'Puritanism, Arminianism and Counter-Revolution', in *Origins of the English Civil War*, ed. Conrad Russell (New York: Macmillan, 1973), p. 145.

Tyerman, Luke. *The Life and Times of the Rev. Samuel Wesley, M.A., Rector of Epworth, and the Father of the Revs. John and Charles Wesley, the Founders of the Methodists* (London: Simpkin, Marshall & Co., 1866).

Vickers, Jason E. 'Charles Wesley's Doctrine of the Holy Spirit: A Vital Resource for the Renewal of Methodism', *Asbury Journal* 61:1 (Spring 2006), 47–60.

Vickers, Jason E. 'Christology', in *The Oxford Handbook of Methodist Studies*, ed. William J. Abraham and James Kirby (Oxford: Oxford University Press, forthcoming in 2009).

Vickers, Jason E. *Invocation and Assent: The Making and Remaking of Trinitarian Theology* (Grand Rapids, MI: Eerdmans, 2008).

von Rohr, John. 'Covenant and Assurance in Early English Puritanism', *Church History* 34 (1965): 195–203.

Wainwright, Geoffrey. 'Why Wesley was a Trinitarian' in *Methodists in Dialogue*, ed. G. Wainwright (Nashville, TN: Kingswood Books, 1995), pp. 261–76.

Walker. *The Covenant of Grace, in Nine Sermons* (London, 1788).

Walmsley, Robert. 'John Wesley's Parents: Quarrel and Reconciliation', *Proceedings of the Wesley Historical Society* 29 (1953): 50–7.

Walsh, John. ' "Methodism" and the Origins of English-Speaking Evangelicalism', in *Evangelicalism: Comparative Studies of Popular Protestantism in North America, the British Isles, and Beyond, 1700–1900*, ed. Mark A. Noll, David W. Bebbington and George A. Rawlyk (New York: Oxford University Press, 1994), p. 23.

Walsh, John and Taylor, Stephen. 'The Church and Anglicanism in the "Long" Eighteenth Century', in *The Church of England, c. 1689–c. 1833: From Toleration to Tractarianism*, ed. John Walsh, Colin Haydon, and Stephen Taylor (Cambridge: Cambridge University Press, 1993), pp. 16–17.

Waterman, A. M. C. 'The Nexus between Theology and Political Doctrine in Church and Dissent', in *Enlightenment and Religion: Rational Dissent in Eighteenth-Century Britain*, ed. Knud Haakonssen (New York: Cambridge University Press, 1996), pp. 193–218.

Weber, Theodore R. *Politics in the Order of Salvation: Transforming Wesleyan Political Ethics* (Nashville, TN: Kingswood Books, 2001).

Wigger, John. *Taking Heaven by Storm: Methodism and the Rise of Popular Christianity in America* (New York: Oxford University Press, 1998).

Young, B. W. *Religion and Enlightenment in Eighteenth Century England: Theological Debate from Locke to Burke* (Oxford: Clarendon Press, 1998).

Zachman, Randall. *The Assurance of Faith: Conscience in the Theology of Martin Luther and John Calvin* (Louisville, KY: Westminster John Knox Press, 2005).

INDEX

INDEX

God 8, 11, 13, 19, 32, 40–1, 54–5, 58,
  60, 62–3, 68, 72, 76, 78, 80,
  84–9, 92–3, 95–6, 99–101, 103,
  107–8, 110
Gospel 1–2, 6, 22, 92
grace 85–7, 91, 96, 99–100, 109
Green, V. H. H. 64
Gregory, Jeremy 34–5, 44–5

Halévy, Elie 51
Hanoverian monarchy 9, 62, 65, 70,
  72, 74
Hatch, Nathan O. 73
Heitzenrater, Richard P. 17
Hempton, David 35, 70–4, 76–7
Higden, William 65–6, 72
High Church Tory 2–4, 61–3, 65,
  68–9, 74
holiness 43, 58, 89–90, 98
Holy Club 12, 64
Holy Spirit 13–14, 84, 94–6, 98–9,
  103–4, 106
Hooker, Richard 8, 75
Hopkey, Sophia 13
Horne, George 50
House of Commons 69
House of Hanover 72
House of Lords 75
Howard, Harry L. 70
human liberties 66, 68, 72–4, 76
human nature 68
human rights 64
Hume, David 56
Hutton, James 14
Hynson, Leon O. 64, 66, 68–73, 76–7

iconography 33
image of God 77–9, 88–9
Ireland 6, 20, 26
Irish Methodist 25–6
Islam 81
Islamic states 47

Jacobite 62, 64, 66, 68–9, 71–2
Jacobitism 20–1, 65, 72
James II 62
Jennings, Theodore W. 71, 73–4, 76–7

Jesus Christ 1–2, 13–14, 23, 37, 58, 60,
  84, 86, 90–7, 99, 106–7
Johnson, Samuel 51
Julian calendar 9
justification 21, 58, 92–3, 101

Kempis', Thomas a 11
Kingswood school 18, 39
Knox, James 58

law of nature 68
Law, William 64–5, 84
lay preaching 41
liberty 26, 67–8, 72, 74, 77–8, 89
Lincoln College 11
Lincolnshire 10
Locke, John 42
logic of prevenience 109
logic of subordination 13, 19
Long, D. Stephen 81
Lord's Supper 100
Louis XIV 47
Luther, Martin 14, 90

Marxist 74
Maryland 25
means of grace 15, 29, 55, 100–1, 106
Methodism 5, 16, 24–5, 27–8, 33, 48–9,
  55, 61, 73, 87
Methodist 3, 6, 10, 12, 17, 20–3, 25–30,
  32, 34, 47–9, 52–3, 56, 60, 63, 66,
  72–3, 80, 102, 109–10
Methodist Episcopal Church in
  America 29
Metropolitan Church 8
Middlesex 69
Middleton, Conyers 57
Model Deed 23
Molther, Philipp Heinrich 15
monarchianism 107
monarchy 3
Moore, Henry 34
moral law 76, 88, 90
Moravian 13, 15–16, 20, 25, 57
Mosaic covenant 88
Mosaic law 90
Moses 91